RIOTOUS VICTORIANS

"The Riots in London on Sunday, Nov. 13: Defence of Trafalgar Square"

RIOTOUS
VICTORIANS

by Donald C. Richter

OHIO UNIVERSITY PRESS
Athens   London

Library of Congress Cataloging in Publication Data

Richter, Donald C   1934–
   Riotous Victorians.

   Bibliography: p. 171
   Includes index.
   1. Riots—England—History—19th century. 2. Demonstrations—
England—History—19th century. 3. Great Britain—History—
Victoria, 1837–1901.
I. Title.
HV 6485.G72E57   303.6'2   80-25055
ISBN 0-8214-0571-3
ISBN 0-8214-0618-3 pbk.

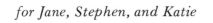

for Jane, Stephen, and Katie

CONTENTS

LIST OF ILLUSTRATIONS

THE HOME SECRETARIES AND PERMANENT UNDER SECRETARIES

The Home Secretaries—1866–1892

Spencer Walpole . . . . 6 July 1866

Gathorne-Hardy . . . . 17 May 1867

Henry Bruce . . . . .9 December 1868

Robert Lowe. . . . . 9 August 1873

Sir Richard Cross. . . . . 21 February 1874

Sir William Harcourt . . . . .23 April 1880

Sir Richard Cross. . . . . .24 June 1885

H.C.E. Childers . . . . 6 February 1886

Henry Matthews . . . . .3 August 1886

Herbert Asquith . . . . 18 August 1892

Permanent Under Secretaries

Horatio Waddington . . . . 15 May 1848

Adolphus Liddell. . . . . 14 August 1867

Godfrey Lushington . . . . 25 July 1885

NOTE ON THE ARCHIVES

The vast bulk of the materials on the Home Office is found either with the papers of the individual Home Secretary or at the Public Record Office. The former source varies in value according to the whims of the man and his successors. The papers of Spencer Walpole and Henry Matthews are lost; Hardy's papers are available at the Ipswich and East Suffolk Record Office, Lowe's (Lowe states in his autobiography that he "kept no correspondence"), in private hands, Cross' in the British Museum and in perfect order and arrangement; Harcourt's papers dangerously heaped in large storage boxes in a second-floor unfinished room of an annex building on the grounds of Stanton Harcourt. Childers' papers were for the most part destroyed by enemy action during the war, but fragments survive at the Commonwealth Society, and the Asquith papers are in the Bodleian at Oxford. The official papers which remained at the Home Office grew to such unwieldly proportions that by 1872 a decision was made to send the papers deemed historical to the Public Record Office. By 1880 the P.R.O. itself could no longer absorb the increasing enormity, and by virtue of the powers to "destroy" papers in its safe-keeping, given in 1877 (PRO Act), the P.R.O. began to weed in the Home Office files, subject to H.O. approval. In 1883 Harcourt gave permission to the P.R.O. to determine which documents might be destroyed at the expiration of a given time, and without further H.O. knowledge or approval.[1] In spite of this, an astounding number of reports, papers, memos, letters, and correspondence survives at the P.R.O. in Chancery Lane and Kew Gardens.

---

1. P.R.O. MEPO 2/33.

1

THE FORCES OF RIOT CONTROL

One of the most prevalent misconceptions of English history may well be the alleged public orderliness of late Victorian society. We have come to think of the Victorians as a peaceable, law-abiding people, orderly and circumspect, at least in public. The words "mob" and "riot" are not easily associated with Victorian England. As recently as 1967 F.C. Mather felt able to write of the "conquest of mob disorder" and "the elimination of riot" from mid-nineteenth century England.[1] But the Victorian mob was real and potentially extremely dangerous.

The mob violence found in later Victorian England was but the sequel to a long heritage of violence. Rowdiness and resistance to authority, virtually endemic in the English character, had been nurtured by centuries of national independence and political intransigence. Eric Hobsbawm, in his study of secret societies, peasant revolutionaries, and mob riots, took the view that these were primitive and archaic social survivals. Their incidence in England in the nineteenth and twentieth centuries stemmed from the period before the masses were brought within the pale of the Constitution. These peoples had been newly catapulted into political consciousness and an industrialized society. As far as England was concerned, Hobsbawm pointed to 1850 as about the time the industrial population learned the modern "rule of the game." This was not to say that they always obeyed these rules, for "it must not be forgotten that the bulk of industrial workers... began as first-generation immigrants from pre-industrial societies,... and they looked back as much as forwards."[2] The past to which these Victorians looked back was replete with lawlessness, violence, and riot.

That disorderly conduct was part of the warp and woof of the life of the English common people is evidenced in the lengthy catalogue of incidents spanning several centuries. In the early nineteenth century there were the Rebecca Riots of southwestern Wales,[3] the "Last Labourers' Revolt" of 1830, the Bristol Riots of 1831, the Plug-Plot Riots of 1842 in Lancashire and Yorkshire especially, the Birmingham Bull Ring Riot of 1839, frequent anti-Poor Law Riots subsequent to 1834, the severe disturbances preceding the passage of the first Reform Bill in Birmingham, Nottingham, Bristol and other cities; the many Luddite disturbances and later the Chartist uprisings. These were only the more spectacular disturbances. Rural life was notoriously tumultuous. In 1839 a Welsh M.P. begged the Home Secretary for barracks and troops: "A more lawless set of men than the colliers and miners do not exist....It requires some courage to live among a set of savages."[4]

In the late eighteenth century there were the Priestley Riots in Birmingham (1791) and before that the famous Gordon Riots which wracked the Metropolis for ten days, bringing death or injury to 458 persons, and causing untold property damage.[5] Less spectacular, yet for that very reason perhaps even more indicative of the prevalence of mob violence were the customary election riots, the frequent no-popery riots, and the countless mob attacks on John Wesley's preachers, which persisted for over twenty-five years. Robert Wearmouth, a leading authority on social Methodism, lists hundreds of riots of every conceivable type year-by-year from 1740 to 1800. He notes twenty-four riots in 1766 alone.[6] The disorderly strain in British life is clearly traceable back into the seventeenth century. Max Beloff, in his *Public Order and Popular Disturbances 1660–1714,* found the later Stuart period rampant with church brawling, disorderly alehouses, Maypole battles, riotous public executions, debaucheries at fairs, attacks upon police, and many pointless, spontaneous riots.[7]

One of the less fortunate concomitants of the almost fanatical English devotion to liberty was the staunch opposition to the establishment of any effective police authority, which resulted in totally inadequate policing until the mid-nineteenth century. The pervasive impunity afforded by the absence of effective forces of

law and order contributed handsomely to the heritage of crowd
violence.

In the Middle Ages the hopes of law and order rested theoretically on the shoulders of the general public. Anglo-Saxon principle
overly optimistically held every citizen responsible for the maintenance of the local peace. Every resident of a tithing was expected to aid the shire-reeve (later called sheriff) in apprehending
law-breakers. As tithings were combined into hundreds, special
responsibility devolved upon the deputy of the hundred, who in
some places was a paid officer, but the concept of community
responsibility was retained. By the middle of the fourteenth
century, the ecclesiastical parish had replaced the feudal hundred
as the rural unit of government, and the parish constable had
largely replaced the deputy of the hundred. Rural policing remained under local control in the persons of the Justices of the
Peace and the Lords Lieutenant. What this all meant was that no
national police system ever took root in England and to this day
seems in principle unacceptable.[8] The parish constabulary, largely
unpaid and wholly untrained, remained the chief law enforcement
agency well into the nineteenth century.

Urban policing began as early as 1285 when the Statute of
Westminster regularized a practice known as the Watch and Ward.
Appointed by the town guild, this citizen patrol was primarily
intended to watch for fires and to prevent crimes. Terence's
ancient epigram "Who's to guard the guard?" became a modern
dilemma as many borough nightwatchmen, poorly paid and
nonprofessional, turned out to be rogues themselves. By the
eighteenth century collusion became common and the wealthy
resorted to armed servants of their own.[9] As the constabulary
system broke down, alternative haphazard schemes burgeoned in
many boroughs; over five hundred private "Prosecution Societies"
were established.[10] Two magistrates of London's Bow Street
Station, the novelist Henry Fielding and his blind half-brother
Sir John Fielding (whose home was later to be burnt to the ground
during the Gordon Riots), concocted various schemes for crime
prevention in the Bow Street neighborhood. They implemented a
street patrol of citizen-householders, actually bands of "thief-
takers" aided by local informers. Despite the acknowledged success of the Bow Street Runners, as the patrols came to be called,

public suspicions effectively scotched all suggestions to extend this and other fledgling police forces to all of London.[11] Another magistrate, Dr. Patrick Colquhoun, wrote persuasively of the importance of police *prevention* of crime and the intelligent coordination of police efforts, and was for the most part ignored. The English public and judiciary seemed to place a greater confidence in barbarous punishments of the comparatively few lawbreakers who were amateurish and/or careless enough to get caught.

The coincidence of inadequate policing, increasing individual lawlessness, and the severe economic dislocations of the early decades of the nineteenth century meant an alarming increase in rioting and public disorder. Between 1780 and 1820 five Parliamentary Commissions of inquiry investigated this problem without presenting a bill to Parliament.[12] The disorders attending the return of Queen Caroline to England provoked Wellington to demand the establishment of a police force for London "without a moment's delay."[13] Robert Peel, deeply influenced by Colquhoun, took steps to implement plans of such a force the very month of his appointment as Home Secretary (January 1822), but his plans were summarily rejected by Peel's own Special Commission on grounds that an effective police would be irreconcilable with "that perfect freedom of action and exemption from interference which are the great privileges and blessings of society in this country."[14] Even such highminded reformers as Romilly and Mackintosh long opposed the establishment of police forces. For over a century the Whig party had consistently opposed the creation of any police force anywhere. John Fielden, Thomas Wakley and Thomas Slingsby Duncombe led the radical opposition to police reform.[15]

The Metropolitan Police Act of 1829,[16] nebulous and deficient as it proved to be, was nevertheless a testimony to Peel's indefatigable effort and political patience. The legal powers of the new constables were left perilously vague or even undefined as were the jurisdiction and province of the two pioneer Magistrates, Sir Charles Rowan and Sir Richard Mayne. Problems of morale surfaced quickly. Constabulary pay of nineteen shillings weekly quite predictably attracted other than the most desirable applicants. Recuits were on duty eight hours a day, six days a week. In

1868 their time off duty was reduced to two days a month, one of which was a Sunday, an arrangement both Superintendent Henderson and Lord Harcourt as Home Secretary still considered "fairly liberal" in 1882.[17] Less serious annoyances plagued the fledgling organization: in its first months a Sergeant was dismissed "for having lost or made away with part of his clothing."[18] General instructions inculcated the necessity for courteous, ever-respectful police behavior in the face of anticipated public suspicion and hostility. The carrying of truncheons instead of guns or cutlasses and the choice of a blue color for the uniforms were designed to dissociate the new police from the military.[19]

The initial force of 3,314 men (as of June 1, 1830) suffered open hostility from the populace on the streets, cruel and inaccurate misrepresentations in the press, blatant misjudgments at the hands of juries, and even obstructiveness on the part of both Whig and Tory Home Secretaries. The Cold Bath Fields riot of 1833, in which one constable was killed and two others stabbed, was the most serious of many confrontations, but it also marked the turning of the public tide toward a growing respect. By the end of 1833 London's "bobbies" had effectively proven they could combat rioting without military aid. The Metropolitan force soon became the most efficient law enforcement organization in the country.[20]

The Municipal Corporations Act of 1835 not only reconstituted most urban governmental structures, but also required all boroughs regardless of size to establish some form of police system administered by a Watch Committee to be paid for out of local rates. The Metropolitan Police received a flood of requests for assistance from some two hundred boroughs and responded by sending out experienced men at all levels to these fledgling forces. The vast majority of borough forces thus imitated Scotland Yard in organization, but many were too small for similar effectiveness. Many boroughs employed their paupers as constables the better to husband municipal funds.[21]

The rural areas of England were the slowest in developing even the most rudimentary form of police protection. Following the establishment of the Metropolitan and borough forces, large numbers of law-breakers migrated to or sought refuge in the counties.[22] County magistrates increasingly came to rely on the willingness of the Metropolitan force to send out contingents to the provinces not only in time of actual disorder, but also for races, elections, public meetings, and other occasions of potential disorder. By the late 1830's this escalating demand began to strain the manpower resources of Scotland Yard. A Royal Commission, including Rowan and the ubiquitous Chadwick, urged the Government to take immediate positive action on rural policing. Once again informed advice proved less persuasive than threats of violence and in the end it was the Chartist disorders which induced Parliament to pass in one month the County Police Act of 1839.[23] The Act only permitted and did not compel the counties to establish police forces; it is more commonly known as the Permissive Act. Unlike the relatively uniform borough forces, the few counties taking advantage of the Act established their police organizations entirely along individual lines, some emulating the Irish Constabulary. Few of the police in these counties had been trained by the Metropolitan force. The Home Office reserved only the right to ratify appointments of Chief Constables. Because the central government contributed no funds for this purpose, most counties took no action whatever. Of the fifty-two counties of England and Wales, only fifteen had established forces of any kind by the end of 1840, and only twenty-two by 1853.[24]

A Select Committee of 1853 acknowledged the Permissive Act to be a failure and its recommendations indirectly formed the basis of the County and Borough Police Forces Act of 1856, commonly known as the Obligatory Act. This Act compelled all counties in England and Wales (and in 1857, in Scotland) to organize police forces, the Government providing one-fourth the costs of salary and uniforms (for both county and borough forces). For the first time local government acquiesced to the principle of central administrative control in the matter of policing, because the grant was made conditional on acceptable reports by Her Majesty's Inspectors of Constabulary. Jenifer Hart has shown that even after the passage of the Obligatory Act, the standards of policy remained low in many boroughs.[25] Improvement came, but only gradually. The Inspectors found 120 deficient forces in 1857, seventy-eight in 1860. There were 1,830 vacancies in 1866 and Lord Wodehouse worried that "the force is melting away."[26] It was not till 1890 that the Inspectors reported no deficient forces.

A further facet of police weakness lay in its fragmented and decentralized organization. In 1857 there were 239 entirely separate forces in England and Wales alone, a great many of them simply too small to perform their role effectively. After 1888, at the repeated urging of Parliament, some amalgamation did take place, but as late as 1908 there were still 193 distinct forces, 125 in 1967.[27] The Local Government Act of 1888 fostered greater administrative efficiency by prescribing Standing Joint Committees composed of both county councillors and magistrates in all counties, to serve uniformly as the ultimate county police authority. The same Act increased Parliamentary financial support for county forces to one-half the cost of pay and uniforms.

In general, rural forces proved inferior to the urban both in effectiveness and in numbers. In 1885 the proportion of police to population was twice as high in urban areas as in the counties. Where cities such as Liverpool, Manchester, Edinburgh, and Glasgow showed proportions of 1 to 555, 1 to 406, 1 to 588, and 1 to 569 respectively; in the southern counties the ratio was 1 to 1,110, in the northern counties 1 to 918, and in North Wales and the the Midlands 1 to 1,146.[28] By 1908 the total number of police serving the United Kingdom stood at 45,000, giving an approximate ratio of 1 to 1,000.[29] In contrast the ratio in 1967 stood at 1 to 556 for all Britain, 1 to 730 in rural areas, 1 to 375 in greater London, and 1 to 510 in other urban areas.[30]

Until 1907 there existed no provisions for any professional training, and pay rates tended to discourage the educated. In 1867 the Metropolitan force of over 7,000 boasted only three educated officers, a situation Hardy found absurd.[31] Among the qualifications listed by Childers in 1886: sergeants and constables, ability to read and write; Superintendants or Inspectors, ability "to read and write well."[32] A Royal Commission upon the Duties of the Metropolitan Police (1906–1908) first published the glaring anomaly between the legally and psychologically appropriate behavior expected of police and their utter lack of any technical training. Sir Edward Henry in 1907 spearheaded the first such school, suitably called Peel House, designed to provide a ten weeks course to three hundred men at a time.[33]

While the British police forces provided by these Acts constituted a vast improvement over the system prevailing before 1829 and proved sufficient for most ordinary police work, most still remained inadequate in the face of mob disorder of any kind. At the height of the controversy over the Cleator Moor riot of 1884 the Home Secretary explained "In Ireland, where there is a constant state of semi-civil war going on, there are plenty of police available; but in England we are not in the habit of having 1,000 men constantly ready to deal with a Salvation Army or a Skeleton Army, or with processions of Catholics or Orangemen."[34] In the wake of the West End riots of February 1886, a Member of Parliament was able to describe even the Metropolitan force as "...admirably organized for the preservation of the ordinary peace of the Metropolis...but they were unprepared for what was really the strategical duty of dealing with large disorderly crowds."[35] Almost two decades later, the situation remained quite the same. The Chief Constable of Nottinghamshire testified before a Select Committee in 1908 that "the police force of the whole Kingdom is only just sufficient to perform the ordinary police duty; there is no reserve at all, you understand."[36]

One redeeming practice, which in times of emergency might salvage something of public order, was the borrowing of police contingents from neighboring forces. The Police Act of 1890 specifically authorized and urged voluntary standing agreements for mutual aid among neighboring boroughs and counties, but by 1908, of a total 192 separate police forces in England and Wales, only thirty counties and twenty-seven boroughs had signed such agreements.[37] The theory was in one respect impractical in that a riot serious enough to warrant such emergency borrowing might logically be expected to threaten also those places whose police forces were thus depleted. For instance, in the late summer of 1893, while 259 borrowed constables guarded the crowds at the Doncaster races under this type of agreement, striking miners from the constables' own home towns suddenly broke out in rampant violence which lasted almost a week and ended in fatality and great property damage.[38] For this reason in times of emergency most authorities were very reluctant to volunteer their own forces, and, of course, there were no means of coercing them to do so.

Nor did availability of adequate control forces invariably insure maintenance of the peace. In 1871 Sir Charles Dilke delivered a republican lecture at the Temperance Hall at Bolton during which Tory crowds tried to storm the meeting and there was a general melee in which one man was killed. Bolton magistrates had augmented their own eighty police by fifty County constables. However, except for a sergeant and three constables posted outside the hall, the large force had been stationed out of sight so as not to provoke the crowds and was not called in until the riot was well under way. The Liberals charged that the Conservative magistrates had purposefully delayed in calling the police in order to withhold protection from Dilke, but a Home Office inquiry by Bruce fully exonerated the Bolton magistrates of any intentional wrongdoing.[39]

Another alternative was the swearing in of special constables to deal with extraordinary situations, a practice regularized by the Special Constables Act of 1931. During the last Chartist scare of 1848, London authorities deputized 170,000 special constables to supplement the regular police and military reserves, but the former were not actually utilized.[40] During the great Fenian scare of 1867-8 over 100,000 special constables served throughout the country, and in the wake of Bloody Sunday, 1887, over thirty thousand Londoners volunteered for special duty.[41] Despite such popular enthusiasm this device involved distinct disadvantages. Local ratepayers had to pay the special constables, a feature which commended the practice to Home Secretaries but which discouraged local authorities. A band of hastily gathered specials were, not surprisingly, far less efficient a deterrent force than either police or military. A distraught mayor of Exeter explained:

> ...every City in the Kingdom is at the mercy of the Roughs of each City for a time if on any pretext they choose suddenly to combine and nothing is easier than to get them together for purposes of mischief. Special Constables are of no great avail in any sudden tumult, even if they are got together and sworn in there is no means of distinguishing them in a dark night from the Roughs and if they do not fight each other, they do not act much in concert.[42]

Under these circumstances the beleaguered British magistrate looked quickly enough to the military as an easy resort. As Max Beloff has shown, it was the ordinary course of action during the later Stuart period.[43] In 1715 Jacobite rioting had prompted the Whigs to pass the Riot Act which allowed the dispersion by military force of crowds of more than twelve persons who refused to disperse voluntarily when so ordered by lawful authority. In the nineteenth century, it became customary for magistrates to read the Riot Act as a legal preliminary to calling in the military, and it was usually not until this flashpoint had been reached that the Home Office became involved as the Government department responsible for all areas of domestic peace. The easy cases were dealt with at the local level; only the difficult ever reached the Home Office. The more delicate the circumstances the greater the probability of referral for advice to the Home Secretary. Frequently the Home Office would not be informed of a local police problem until the situation was already quite dangerous.

The Home Office has with ample reason been characterized as the hot-seat of the Government. Next only to the Prime Ministership (which Lord Randolph Churchill once called a "dunghill"), the Home Office was easily the most sensitive post in the cabinet.[44] The routine responsibilities alone were enough to daunt the most capable of administrators while emergency situations might claim his entire attention without warning. Hardy described it as an office where "...failures are at once detected, and one works in a glass hive."[45] "The eyes of the people are never off the unlucky Home Secretary," as a letter to the editor of *The Daily News* phrased it in 1871 (10 October). At Cross' appointment the Permanent Under Secretary greeted him with a friendly warning: "The Home Office is the 100 yards target which every fellow fires his shot at and thinks he can hit, so you must be prepared for a little peppering occasionally."[46] Even in the best of times, correct execution of the office's many varied obligations was fraught with hazards and pitfalls—legal, social, political. "A bad thing to be Home Secretary," was Harcourt's terse verdict, and Gladstone's personal secretary Hamilton refers in his wonderfully informative diary to "the detested Home Office."[47] Even Asquith admitted there was enough work "to satisfy the most voracious appetite for work" and he left with the remark, "it was with a sigh of relief... that I laid down my thankless task."[48]

Few Home Secretaries survived the trials of the office to rise higher. Not all fared as badly as the unfortunate Walpole or Childers, but no Home Secretary between Palmerston in 1852 and Asquith in 1892 advanced to the Prime Ministership.

The range of routine obligations and decisions demanded of the Home Secretary was so wide that not even a Victorian administrator could be said to be adequately prepared to cope with each one of so many diverse responsibilities. Were it not for the permanent staff, the job would have been an impossible one. No Home Secretary considered his professional permanent staff adequate to the legal and technical advice he required. The Home Secretary had two Parliamentary Under Secretaries to advise him and one Permanent Under Secretary, a civil service post filled during this period by three experienced hands, Horatio Waddington, Adolphus Liddell, and Godfrey Lushington.

The clerical staff handled the purely routine day-to-day business, calculated in 1885 at 47,000 pieces of incoming correspondence a year, or about 150 per working day, each requiring a written minute and most a responding letter. So much of the day-to-day business was taken care of by the permanent staff that Liddell was able to write to Cross in 1883 "The Boss [Harcourt] is busy over London Gov't—we hardly ever see him."[49]

By far the most perplexing responsibility of the office was the simultaneous preservation of order and protection of all citizens' rights of freedom of speech and freedom to assemble, petition, and demonstrate. It was the Home Secretary who ultimately had to make the difficult decision whether to ban or not to ban meetings, processions, demonstrations and the like, balancing the competing demands of free speech with the demands of order, always keenly aware of the instant political consequences of the slightest misjudgment. The spectre of St. Peter's Field was ever present. If the demonstration was prohibited on unsound legal grounds, the government faced certain public censure. Likewise, if demonstrations were allowed but became disorderly or violent, the government faced political censure from the opposing side. It was a limp tightrope the Home Secretary had to walk again and again, and it is not surprising that slips occurred from time to time. Nor was much help forthcoming from the Prime Minister. Gladstone recalled that Palmerston read the Foreign Office and War Office correspondence and "...let the others rust and rot."[50] Gladstone himself offered scarcely any real assistance to his various Home Secretaries and in the eighties was absolutely preoccupied by Ireland. Disraeli offered not much more in the way of advice. While Home Secretary, Melbourne recalled William IV writing "endless agitated letters urging him...to increase the legal penalties for rioting, to call out the military...."[51] Similarly illiberal advice from Queen Victoria complicated the decision-making process of most of her Home Secretaries.

Faced with a breakdown of law and order, the Home Office first reminded magistrates that responsibility for the preservation of order was a local one and that if the regular police seemed inadequate the proper course was either to borrow police or to swear in special constables. Only as a last resort would the Home Office permit military intervention.

A typical sequence of events may be illustrated from a relatively simple case. Upon application for troops from the mayor of Chippenham in 1865, the Home Office transmitted the letter to the neighboring county's Chief Constable, alerted the appropriate military detachment to stand in readiness for possible services, and replied to the mayor:

> ...You should strengthen the permanent Police of the Borough by swearing in an adequate number of Special Constables and it will also be proper that you should endeavor to obtain assistance from the Chief Constable of Wiltshire. If after these precautions have been taken, you should be of the opinion that the Force at your disposal is insufficient to prevent a disturbance of the peace and further assistance is required which however Sir G.G. [Grey] trusts will not be the case, you should communicate with this office by telegram.[52]

It was not uncustomary for the Home Office to refuse troops upon first application. Even after sending the troops upon second application, as at Lincoln in 1865, Walpole stated:

> Sir George Grey thinks it right to impress upon the magistrates that it is only after all the means of maintaining order and suppressing any riot by the Civil Power have been had recourse to and found insufficient, that Military aid should be resorted to, and the troops be called upon to act.[53]

Hardy refused troops to Cardiff in 1867 indicating that "first resort" ought always to be the swearing in of special constables.[54]

The military units most commonly delegated by the War Office to act in aid of the Civil power came from the Regular Forces, but the law also allowed use of the Auxiliary. The Regular or Local Militia might be called out by proclamation to suppress domestic insurrection (42 Geo. III, 90, 111). The Enrolled Pensioners might be called out with the Home Secretary's warrant by a county Lord Lieutenant or Chief Magistrate to suppress invasion or riot usually for a period not exceeding twelve days (6 and 7 Vict. 95). The Yeomanry and the Volunteers served to repress both foreign invasion and local tumult but served only voluntarily for the latter purpose (44 Geo. III, 54). All these units acted in military organization and were liable to the Mutiny Act and Articles of War.[55]

This divided responsibility accounted for some delays as in 1866 when Manchester magistrates found both the Home Office and the War Office deferring to each other a decision on arming the Pensioners. "This is circumlocution with a vengeance," admitted Walpole. "We send complaints to the War Office, and they send similar complaints to us, and nothing is done by any one. It is time to put an end to this state of things."[56]

During the widespread bread and meat riots in Dorset and Devon in the autumn of 1867 magistrates requested the services of the local Coast Guard contingents. In November looting mobs had been contained in Exeter and Torquay by the use of special constables and Hardy had taken pains to congratulate those authorities on their "determination to maintain order within the Town without resort to military force."[57] However, as the disturbances spread to Newton Abbot, South Molton, and Lyme Regis, appeals for the nearby Coast Guard mounted. The Admiralty had initially forbidden such service and Hardy concurred, although on November 15 the Coast Guard did use armed force to suppress the rioting in Lyme Regis. "The aiding of the Civil Power to the neglect of their ordinary duty is not to be expected of the Coast Guard..." Hardy steadfastly refused.[58]

On occasions when military aid was granted, the Home Office would communicate with the Quarter Master General, Horse Guards, or a Major General who would in turn request HRH the Field Marshal Commander-in-Chief to order the actual troop movements. Theoretically such movements could not be authorized until the actual outbreak of disorder, but in practice troops were commonly transported and held in readiness in some appropriate place close to the scene of the expected disturbance.[59]

Inevitably there were certain legal and practical ambiguities in the relationship between the military officer in charge and the magistrate who called for military assistance. Hardy worked out the following formula, itself somewhat nebulous: "The Military are entirely subordinate to the Civil Power, but the Military officer in charge of a Party is solely in command over his own force and disposes it according to his Military orders or to the best of his judgment in the execution of his duty which may be entrusted to him by the Civil Power." Hardy added that the magistrate ought to remain close by the side of the military officer.[60] In many circumstances this might be an undue hardship on a magistrate. In 1893 a Hull magistrate was excused from such duty on the grounds of conflict of interest as he was also likely to sit in judgment on persons arrested.[61] In London it was customary for magistrates to accompany troops on a rotation basis. In 1886 the Commissioner of the Metropolitan Police was asked whether police had power to call upon the military directly if faced with sudden and uncontrolled rioting. Henderson's reply: "Bringing soldiers on the scene is a very troublesome operation, because you cannot use them unless you have a magistrate, and a magistrate can do nothing unless he reads the Riot Act; and properly speaking the police have no business going to the military authorities; they ought to go to the Home Secretary and the Home Secretary to the military authorities. Therefore if an emergency of that sort arose I think the police would have to face it themselves."[62]

Almost invariably, the use of troops for crowd control proved most undesirable. Soldiers showed themselves extremely reluctant to coerce fellow Britishers, much less fire upon them, but in spite of this the public greatly resented on principle the confrontation of an unarmed citizens' gathering and an armed military force. When called upon to play the role of a policeman the soldier's lot was no happier than that of the Cornish Sergeant dealing with the Pirates of Penzance. For these reasons the intervention of the military more frequently exacerbated than assuaged public unrest. The unfortunate consequences of the use of the military during the Gordon Riots of 1780 and at the Peterloo incident in 1819 continued to haunt magistrates throughout the nineteenth century. In June 1869, Welsh colliers of Mold stoned a military escort of prisoners and the soldiers opened fire killing four, a rare occurrence. A Home Office inquiry absolved the military of all blame.[63] In the wake of the Featherstone Riots in 1893, an interdepartmental committee conducted an investigation as to the effectiveness of existing provisions for coping with widespread rioting. It advised that the Chief Constable, not the magistrates, make the requests for military aid directly to the ranking military officer in the locality. The committee added a warning:

> The most important principle...is, that the calling out of the military to aid in the suppression of rioting should never be resorted to except as a last expedient when there is serious ground for believing that the resources of the civil power will be insufficient; and on this account every possible arrangement should be made beforehand to enable the civil authorities to cope with rioters by means of the constabulary alone.[64]

In 1908 a Select Committee reviewed the 1895 Report and concluded that its directives were clear, well defined, and adequate. The members thought it necessary to reiterate emphatically that the civil authorities were responsible for the preservation of the peace, and that this was to be done primarily with police forces. The Report specifically discouraged the use of the military except in gravest emergency.[65]

When dealing with disorderly crowds British policy of the late Victorian era displayed a patience and forebearance bordering on permissiveness. In most cases, police actually charged crowds only after repeated warning or in self-defense. Customarily the mob attacked the police with far greater zeal and more formidable weapons than the police attacked the people. Armed with only batons, police relied for protection primarily on the iron supports embedded in their top hats, and after 1864 on the helmets which replaced them. Certainly the Victorian mob entertained little, if any, fear of police brutality.

In the wake of the Pall Mall affair of 1886,[66] Henderson admitted that his Police:

> ...are very much afraid of showing too much zeal, because they know perfectly well that the public is quite ready to say if there is a disturbance that they provoked it, and they have always been taught to show the utmost forebearance that can be expected of any Englishman. I am sure I saw the mob that very day treat them in such a way that it is only a marvel to me that they stood it....That is one of our difficulties at all these public meetings; we are bound to show as few police as possible—it produces excitement and irritation, and directly you show police you get a bigger crowd than ever.[67]

During the "Bloody Sunday" riot (1887) a *Globe* reporter saw many sections of the crowd in Trafalgar Square applauding not only the troops, but also the police constables.[68] A visiting American who watched the entire affair from the steps of the National Liberal Club, and who had also been present at the Chicago anarchist riots of the same year, noted that "the much abused London police showed a spirit of moderation towards the mob which they would not receive in any American city."[69] In the smaller towns police were less prone to act so patiently, but they might be just as likely to join the fracas as to act to suppress it.

Judicial sentences also reflected this prevailing leniency, especially noticeable when contrasted with the harsh punishments meted out during the first half of the nineteenth century. Under the prodding of Romilly, Mackintosh, and Peel, most of the egregiously Draconian penalties had disappeared by the forties. The suppression of the Labourers' Revolt of 1830 demonstrated the early severity of the law against rioters. Though the rioting had swept through sixteen counties from Kent to northern Wales, and there was much rickburning and wrecking of threshing machines, the starving laborers committed very little personal violence. But of the 1,406 rioters tried, nine were hanged, 464 transported to Australia, and 657 imprisoned.[70] One of those hanged was a nineteen-year-old youth whose chief offense was that he had hit a prominent financier with a stick and severely damaged his hat.[71] In flagrant contrast, the ringleaders of the Irish mob which beat up Murphy in 1871 received only short prison terms and were released less than one month after Murphy died from the effects of their beating.[72] In 1849 an Irishman who had knifed a policeman received only twenty-one days.[73]

The combination of inadequate forces of repression, a lenient judiciary, and a tolerant, almost nonchalant public attitude contributed to a realm quite fertile for riots of all types.

1. F.C. Mather, *Public Order In the Age of the Chartists*, p.v.

2. Eric Hobsbawm, *Primitive Rebels*, p. 108.

3. David Williams, *The Rebecca Riots: A Study in Agrarian Discontent*.

4. Charles Fay, *Life and Labour In the Nineteenth Century*, p. 185. 4th edition.

5. J. Steven Watson, *The Reign of George III 1760–1815*, pp. 236–239.

6. R.F. Wearmouth, *Methodism and the Common People of the Eighteenth Century*, pp. 32–36, 138–164.

7. Max Beloff, *Public Order and Popular Disturbances 1660–1714*, pp. 20–28.

8. *See London Daily Telegraph,* June 12, 1972.

9. Charles Reith, *A New Study of Police History,* pp. 24, 25.

10. H. Finer, "The Police and Public Safety," in *A Century of Municipal Progress 1835-1935,* edited by Harold Laski, W. Jennings, and William Robson, p. 277.

11. Reith, p. 26; Finer, p. 274.

12. Samuel G. Chapman (ed)., *The Police Heritage In England and America,* p. 13.

13. Reith, p. 122.

14. Ibid., p. 28.

15. F.C. Mather, *Public Order In the Age of the Chartists,* p. 31.

16. George IV. cap. 44.

17. Harcourt to Lord's Day Observance Society, March 9, 1882, P.R.O. HO 45/A 13278.

18. P.R.O. MEPOL 2/36.

19. Nevertheless the epithet "Blue Army" was common during the thirties and forties.

20. See Reith, pp. 121-194.

21. Finer, p. 280.

22. For an opposing view see Jenifer M. Hart, "Reform of the Borough Police 1835-1856," *English Historical Review,* pp. 411-427.

23. 2 & 3 Vict. cap. 93.

24. Chapman, p. 15.

25. Hart, *The British Police* p. 34.

26. Wodehouse to Russell, January 18, 1866, Russell Papers, P.R.O. 30/22/16A/189-93.

27. Chapman, p. 16.

28. Great Britain, *Parliamentary Papers,* Vol. XXXIV (1866), "Police (Counties and Boroughs), Reports of the Inspectors of Constabulary for the Year ending 29th September, 1885."

29. Great Britain, *Parliamentary Papers,* Vol. VII (1908), "Report of the Select Committee on the Employment of Military In Cases of Disturbances," Evidence, Q 247.

30. Chapman, p. 16. The actual number of police in 1967 stood at 81,298.

31. Gathorne Hardy to Disraeli, December 26, 1867, Hughendon Papers, B/XX/4a/16.

32. Rules for County Constabulary (England) April 12, 1886, P.R.O. HO 45/A 50178.

33. Finer, pp. 288, 289.

34. *3 Hansard,* CXCI (1884), 407.

35. Ibid., CCCIII (1886), 1412.

36. "Report...on the Employment of the Military," Evidence, Q 241.

37. Ibid., p. iii of Report.

38. Great Britain, *Parliamentary Papers,* Vol. XVII (1893-1894), "Report of the Committee appointed to enquire into the Circumstances connected with the Disturbances at Featherstone on the 7th of September, 1893."

39. HO 45/9296.

40. *Annual Register* (1848), Chronicle. In addition to the police and special constables there were "Local Constables" (about 600 in 1875) privately hired under 2 & 3 Vict. C 47. They guarded parks, dockyards, public

institutions, theatres, music halls, banks, railroad stations, shops and the like. P.R.O. HO 45/43207.

41. *Annual Register* (1887), p. 177. For the Fenian scare, see Chapter II.

42. Mayor of Exeter to Hardy, November 15, 1867, HO 45/OS 7992.

43. Max Beloff, *Public Order and Popular Disturbances 1660-1714*, pp. 144, 152, 153.

44. Hamilton's Diary, April 17, 1887: B.M. Add. Mss 48646, f. 24.

45. Alfred E. Gathorne-Hardy, *Gathorne-Hardy, 1st Early Cranbrook, A Memoir* Vol. I, p. 216.

46. Liddell to Cross, February 21, 1874, B.M. Add. Mss 51270, f. 125.

47. A.G. Gardiner, *The Life of Sir William Harcourt*, Vol. I, P. 389; Hamilton's Diary, February 1, 1886: B.M. Add. Mss 48642, p. 123.

48. Roy Jenkins, *Life of Asquith*, p. 85; H.H. Asquith, *Fifty Years of Parliament*, Vol. I, p. 210.

49. HO 45/A7070B; Cross Papers, Liddell to Cross, January 13, 1883, B.M. Add. Mss 51273, f. 178.

50. Gladstone Papers, B.M. Add. Mss 44302, f. 145 ff.

51. David Cecil, *Lord M*, p. 42.

52. Bruce to Mayor of Chippenham, October 16, 1865, HO 41/20/272-273.

53. Walpole to Mayor of Lincoln, July 7, 1865, HO 41/20/255.

54. HO 41/21/12.

55. For a fuller discussion, see HO 45/8060.

56. HO 45/7799/169.

57. Hardy to Mayor of Torquay, November 5, 1867, HO 41/21/61.

58. HO 41/21/63. See also HO 45/OS/7992.

59. Walpole to Horse Guards, July 6, 1865, HO 41/20/253.

60. Hardy to Mayor of Salford (Manchester Division), November 6, 1867, HO 41/21/57.

61. HO 45/A54856, "The Duties of His Honor Judge Bedwell and the Hull Strike."

62. Great Britain, *Parliamentary Papers*, Vol. XXXIV (1886), C. 4665, Minutes of Evidence, Q 311, p. 12.

63. HO 45/8240.

64. Great Britain, *Parliamentary Papers*, Vol. XXXV (1895), C 7650, "Report of the Interdepartmental Committee on Riots Appointed By the Home Secretary, May, 1894."

65. "Report on the Employment of the Military," p. iii.

66. See Chapter VIII.

67. Great Britain, *Parliamentary Papers*, Vol. XXXIV (1886), C. 4665. Minutes of Evidence, Q 331, p. 13.

68. *Globe*, November 14, 1887.

69. *The Times*, November 14, 1887.

70. George Rudé, "The Study of Popular Disturbances In the 'Pre-Industrial' Age," *Historical Studies*, X, No. 40 (May 1960), p. 462.

71. G.D.H. Cole, *A Short History of the British Working Class Movements 1789-1947, p. 75.*

72. *3 Hansard*, CCXI (1872), 949 ff., 1725 ff.

73. *4 Hansard*, XXVIII (1894), 261-265.

2

FENIAN TERRORISM IN ENGLAND

The great Fenian scare of the 1860s presented grave problems to both the English police and the Home Office. Dealing with armed terrorists was a totally unfamiliar experience for the ill-equipped police force. The handling of the Fenian problem by the Home Office illustrates the singular care necessary in balancing the requirements of security with the protection of traditional civil rights.

The Irish Catholics resident in England had posed a special concern through the centuries. Since the days of Elizabeth, most English had considered it a part of their patriotic obligation to guard against unrelenting "Papist" conspiracy. For some it was a welcome obligation. Long-buried memories of Gunpowder Plots surfaced easily in times of national crisis and there was always a Titus Oates anxious to identify the real foe. English Protestants peered apprehensively at Catholics from behind the Test Act fortifications. The mere suggestion of any relaxation of this legislation resurrected in a moment the ageless spectres, for example, in 1780, precipitating the worst London rioting of the century. Nineteenth-century Catholic Emancipation, the Oxford Movement, the Tractarian literature, and the Catholic conversions led by Newman and Manning did nothing to allay this persistent Catholophobia. Prompted by the ritualistic controversy which swept through the Church of England, many of the more fervid saw the spectre of Guy Fawkes lurking behind every candlestick and altar. The surplice riots of the forties demonstrated the vehemence of such fears. Even the most seemingly innocuous Papal pronouncements evoked riots, burnings-in-effigy, and legislative retaliation, symptoms of an unrelenting distrust plowed deeply into the English religious landscape.

If English Catholics were mistrusted, the Irish immigrant Catholics were doubly so, bearing a twin liability, religious and political. At annual Orange Day (July 12) celebrations, Protestant victory parades celebrated Ireland's seventeenth century defeat, and the price she paid. In the streets and fields of western England, Wales, and Scotland, the Irish and the Orangemen fought the Battle of the Boyne again and again through the centuries. The English perennially feared an importation of what they considered endemic Irish disorder. Irishmen anywhere were "notoriously inflammable and mercurial."[1]

In 1861 the census showed 601,634 Irish-born immigrants in England and Wales, and 204,003 in Scotland. They did not mix with the general population, but settled clannishly in Irish enclaves, adhering to their own peculiar customs, marrying only among themselves. In the countryside the Irish might well comprise an entire town, as at Cleator Moor (Cumberland), while in the larger cities, they settled in well-defined districts, as at Birmingham, Liverpool, Glasgow, Dundee, in an isolation which tended to perpetuate suspicions and exacerbate disputes between the two camps and rendered the advent of Fenianism especially explosive in its potential.[2]

Organized in America around 1858, the Fenian Brotherhood took its name from a prehistoric and perhaps legendary Irish military force, the Fianna. The aim of the movement was the usual one, an independent Ireland. Absorbing inspiration from Italian nationalist successes and recruits from Irish-American veterans of the American Civil War, the movement spread rapidly on both sides of the Atlantic, though partisans on each side of the water supposed its counterpart was faring better than in reality it was. The story of the doomed and somewhat foolish American Fenian invasions of Canada in 1866, 1870, and 1871 has been told elsewhere,[3] but the real importance of American Fenianism to Ireland lay in the homeland's expectations of abundant financial and arms support from Irish-Americans.

In Ireland the acknowledged leader of the movement was James Stephens, who was wounded in the rebellion of 1848. He had set 1865 as target year for the rising, and, during the autumn of that year, preparations reached a crescendo. Informant tips led to Stephens' arrest in November, and although he managed an escape within a fortnight, his subsequent absence and arrogant behavior cost him the leadership. An informant wrote in 1866, "The friends of Stephens are getting quite disgusted with him for his arbitrary, egotistical, and tyrannical conduct towards anybody that he may have anything to fear from and are falling from him like snow off a ditch."[4] The deadline for the rising having been postponed, arms smuggling, recruitment, and drilling proceeded apace during the early weeks of 1866. Rumors of the most spectacular nature filled the air, and Wodehouse, the Lord Lieutenant, and Fortescue, the Chief Secretary, pressed for extreme measures. Russell hesitated. "There has been hitherto no outbreak," he wrote on January 25. "Is there any proof of a concerted design for insurrection?" By the middle of February, Wodehouse and Fortescue urgently pleaded for suspension of Habeas Corpus as "...indispensible to the safety of the country," and this time Russell concurred. In an unprecedented session on February 17, both houses passed the suspension bill in record time (the vote in Commons: 346 to 6). Even before the passage in the Lords and the signing, the arrests had begun. The repressive effect was almost instantaneous, and the immediate danger seemed to subside. The Queen was always pleased with resolute action, and two days after the arrests, Russell was able to write to Wodehouse, "The Queen entirely approves your conduct in respect to the Fenian conspiracy."[5] The change in government in 1866 had brought Derby in as prime minister for the third time. His choice for the Home Office was Spencer Walpole, the great-grandson of Horatio Walpole. Educated at Eton, Trinity and Lincoln's Inn, Walpole quickly acquired a respected legal reputation. He had entered Commons as a Conservative, first for Midhurst and later for the University of Cambridge. Twice he had held the Home Office, in 1852 and 1858-9, both times for one year or less. His third tenure was to be likewise brief, also less than a year, marked by the two continuing crises, the Fenian conspiracy and the Reform League agitation (see Chapter IV).

What most concerned the Home Office, of course, was Fenian activity in England. Reports of Fenian strength and arms depots in Liverpool and Manchester caused increasing alarm throughout Government circles in 1866 and 1867. Walpole admitted in December 1866, "It seems that the fight is to be in England after all.'"[6] Events of the next few months seemed to bear out Walpole's fears, as the English Fenians, seeing their colleagues in Ireland stymied for the time, attempted to salvage the cause from utter collapse by striking a blow, however hopeless. John McCafferty, one of "Morgan's Raiders" in the American Civil War, a notorious and eccentric Irish adventurer, devised a plan for the storming of Chester Castle with a view to capture of the arms depot, followed by the seizure of the train for Holyhead, its harbor to be used as the jumping off point for an invasion of Ireland. The date fixed was February 11, 1867, but on the day before, an informer learned the details of the plot and conveyed them to the Liverpool police and thence to the government in London. Walpole exchanged hurried telegrams with the mayor of Chester approving the arming of the Volunteers or the Enrolled Pensioners, but ultimately decided the situation required an additional show of force. Through the night of February 10-11 a full battalion of Scots Fusilier Guards was rushed by train from London to Chester. On the morning of the 11th, 1,200 armed Fenians from Liverpool, Manchester, and other towns poured from the train station, milling about and waiting for McCafferty. The prior arrival of the troops made any attack quite impossible and the entire plot was called off. McCafferty himself was delayed on a siding while the troop trains rushed by him. Together with several hundred others, he was captured shortly afterward off the coast of Ireland. He was convicted and sentenced to death, a sentence later commuted to a prison term. The whole escapade ended in a fiasco.[7]

In May 1867, Walpole's mishandling of the Reform League demonstration forced his resignation and he was replaced by Gathorne-Hardy. Born in Staffordshire in 1814, Gathorne-Hardy attended Shrewsbury School, earned a second in Classics at Oriel (Oxford) and was called to the bar at Inner Temple. Considerable success in both law and business paved his way into politics and in 1856 he won a Commons seat as Conservative for Leominster. He served as Under Secretary at the Home Office from 1858 to 1862. In 1865 he defeated Gladstone for one of the University of Oxford seats and joined Derby's third ministry, first as President of the Poor Law Board, and then, upon Walpole's fall, as Home Secretary. His brief tenure at the Home Office was absorbed

Spencer Walpole

Gathorne-Hardy

almost incessantly by the nettlesome Fenian threat which he faced with more than ordinary courage.

A Fenian terrorist campaign of sabotage and incendiarism in England escalated throughout the summer of 1867, striking without warning at gas works, railways, and other public facilities. By sheer chance the Government obtained custody of two Fenians, Thomas Kelly and Timothy Deasy, who were initially arrested as vagrants. Kelly had just replaced Stephens as Chief Executive of the Fenian Brotherhood and had set up headquarters in Manchester, where, with the help of Charles Bradlaugh, he had drawn up an Irish Proclamation of Independence. Considered "much more dangerous—because less scrupulous" than Stephens, Kelly was closely watched at a Manchester jail. "We have caught the leading Fenian of them all," Mayo wrote to Disraeli.[8] The Government's exulting was to be short lived as a daring rescue attempt was quickly organized by Colonel Richard O'Sullivan Burke. A week later, on September 18, Dublin police detectives received word of the plot and telegraphed details to Manchester police and the Home Office. The telegram reached the Manchester police more than an hour before Kelly and Deasy were to be transferred to a county jail, but, nevertheless, the only extra precautions taken were to have a dozen unarmed police accompany the van.

That same afternoon the van transporting Kelly and Deasy was held up by a gang of about thirty to forty armed Fenians who quickly drove off the unarmed police, accidentally killed a police sergeant (Brett) who was inside the van, and rescued both prisoners. The warning telegram which had been sent to the Home Office was delayed there inexplicably so that its own warning to Manchester was not sent till the evening. Hardy, at the time a guest at Balmoral, was actually preparing to give the Queen the good news about the capture of Kelly when he received word of the rescue. "This at Manchester!" he wrote in his diary. "What are we coming to?...The Times is as the public will be ready for strong measures. England will never endure that such an event should happen unpunished." Hardy was especially mortified about the delay at his own office. "I have never been more annoyed," he confided to Mayo.[9]

Kelly and Deasy made good their escape, but police rounded up twenty-nine of the rescuers. The Queen characteristically advised that "some very stringent measures" were appropriate, including an augmented police and a more effective detective bureau. Her Majesty feels, Northcote wrote to Hardy, "that great energy and firmness ought to be displayed by the Government or the consequences will be very serious."[10] In November, five of the accused rescuers were sentenced to death by hanging. Burke was later arrested on another charge, as arms agent, and imprisoned at Clerkenwell.

Irish feelings ran high at news of the death sentences, and there was a rash of demonstrations, mock funerals, and petitions for remission or commutation. Bradlaugh led one of the largest of these outdoor rallies at Clerkenwell Green. Hardy pardoned one prisoner and commuted the sentence of another, but decided to let stand the death sentences for Allen, Larkin, and Gould. As the day of execution approached, a deputation of petitioners from Clerkenwell forced their way into the Home Office, almost reaching Hardy's own inner office. For a time the mob resisted all staff efforts to eject them, threatening "...the blood of these unfortunate men will be upon the Home Secretary. The Home Secretary is this case is the arbiter of life and death, and the blood of these men will never be washed off his hands."[11] The frequently indignant Hardy was this time outraged: "Lawlessness is indeed rife. Stewart [his son] writes in alarm for my personal safety, which must not be purchased by ignominious truckling to those people. The law-loving will stand by a just and proper firmness, and due administration of the law." Two days before the hangings, Hardy defended his position in the House by expressing confidence in the conscientious and skillful decision of the judges in the case, and on Saturday, November 23, amidst an army of police, the due firmness of the law took its course.[12] Assassination threats continued for a time, but Hardy remained stoical, "I am warned of danger and take the precaution of cabs at night, but if real assassins regardless of their safety are after me, what can I do?"[13]

In the wake of the Manchester rescue increasingly concerned appeals were coming in to the Home Office from local authorities across the country; appeals for money, for arms, for troops, for permission to take special precautions. Exeter demanded a national guard and the arming of its police. Berwick-on-Tweed asked for firearms for its four policemen. Cardiff requested revolvers and ammunition. County Derby asked for cutlasses. Differing local circumstances made a uniform, consistent policy all but impossible. In Berwick's case Hardy initially decided that, "...he cannot authorize the issue of Fire Arms to so small a Body of Police. If disturbances are apprehended the Local Authorities should swear in special constables, if they are not prepared to increase the Borough Police." But two days later, upon reapplication, Hardy relented and sent four revolvers with ammunition together with a warning that they are granted "on the understanding that they are to be kept in reserve,... and only entrusted to constables in an emergency or on service of personal danger." Arms given to Lanarkshire's constables "are not to be used by the Police on ordinary duty..." All arms remained the property of the government and were to be returned at the end of twelve months, and ammunition expended charged for at the rate of £1.16.5 per one thousand rounds. Requests for cutlasses were routinely denied: "Cutlasses are not an advisable weapon for use in a crowd as being easily wrested from Constables: The staff is a much better arm." Special constables were enrolled in unprecedented numbers: in October the entire labor force of the Manchester gas works was sworn in. Hardy augmented the Metropolitan Police force by an additional 1,200 men. The Criminal Investigation Department which had been instituted in 1842 furnished detectives for danger spots. Two were in attendance at Preston during the Brett Special Commission, and twelve were sent to Balmoral. In October Hardy wrote to the mayor of Tunbridge urging that Irish immigrants in Kent be watched by police.[14]

In December, Burke and others arranged his own break-out from Clerkenwell, one of the most spectacular prison break attempts of those years. The plan was to blow up the wall of the prison exercise yard during the men's exercise period. Again, it was the Irish Intelligence who through police informers discovered the plot and were able to provide details to the Metropolitan force on December 11: "The plan is to blow up the exercise walls by means of gunpowder, the hour between three and four p.m.; and the signal for 'all right,' a white ball thrown up outside when he is at exercise."[15] In spite of this detailed warning, the plot advanced almost to completion. Extra wardens patrolled

the wall on the twelfth, but Burke exercised as usual in the stipulated yard. The white ball was thrown over the wall and Burke
retreated to a safe corner of the yard, ostensibly to remove something from his shoe. On the outside, police took no notice of a
cask that had been pushed close to the wall, but a woman in the
neighborhood later told of seeing several men attempt to ignite it.
The plot was foiled only by the rescuers' inability to light the fuse,
and they then removed the cask, still unnoticed by the police
patrols. The little white ball had, in fact, been picked up by one
of the sentries! Apparently unaware of its significance, the sentry
kept it for his children.

On the next day, the thirteenth, the cask was again pushed up
adjacent to the wall. This time it was successfully ignited, and the
resulting explosion not only destroyed the two-foot-thick wall,
but demolished tenements on the opposite side of the street,
killed twelve bystanders, and injured 120. One of the police
patrols was so close to the scene at the time that he had most
of his clothes blown off by the force of the explosion. Burke,
however, had no chance to escape, as, on instructions from a
Middlesex Sessions justice, he had been removed to another
exercise yard. But for that precaution, he might have made good
his escape despite the advance warning.

The Clerkenwell explosion swept the country into panic, the
outrage widely interpreted as a signal for a general rising. In an
alarmist atmosphere Disraeli urged Derby to an immediate suspension of Habeas Corpus in England.[16] Derby disagreed: "There
is no doubt that the public are sufficiently alarmed, but not so
much, I think, as to tolerate the Suspension of Habeas Corpus in
England. We must trust to the operation of the ordinary law..."[17]
The Queen's advice was predictable:

> The Queen writes these lines to Mr. Hardy to ask him whether in the
> present state of alarm and panic it would not be really better not to
> delay taking strong measures. Would it not be better to call Parliament
> together for a month—pass the suspension of the Corpus Act for three
> months and then adjourn till the 13th February. What is the use of
> trying to stop these outrages without strong measures to enable us to
> punish these horrid people? And is it right to wait till fresh outrages
> take place and more innocent lives are sacrificed before we resort
> to such measures? The country cries out for protection and the people
> will rally round the Government if it shows courage and energy.[18]

Rumors proliferated of the most dastardly and outlandish Fenian plots: arsenals were to be raided in Colchester, Canterbury, Chelmsford; the Merthyr mine pit-ropes were to be cut; sections of the Lancashire rail line dynamited; the Hull water works sabotaged; and the Shrewsbury railroad station blown up. A ship was on its way from New York carrying thirty men intent on assassinating the Queen and the entire cabinet. Desperately alarmed officials throughout the country rushed arms and munitions to safer depots, set special guards at gaols, banks, factories, warehouses, and public buildings. Having served as a special constable himself during the Chartist scare of 1848, Hardy set great store in them and they were enrolled in the thousands, peaking during the first week of January at 113,674 and not declining substantially till February. Most of the specials were armed only with staves, but Volunteers carried rifles and Hardy gave discretion to local magistrates to authorize their use. The most extraordinary precautions were ordered for London where 53,113 specials operated under the command of a military officer. In the City, seven hundred specials surrounded the Bank of England; eight hundred were at the Post Office. Hardy demanded daily reports from the Commissioner of Police. Engineers from the Board of Works examined all sewers near public buildings; sewer outlets were locked and sentries posted. The Foreign Office ordered wooden shutters for all its first floor windows. Hardy requisitioned chemical lights for emergency installation at strategic points such as Nelson's Column in case the gas lights failed. Instructions were issued to the Horse Guards sentries at Osborne to open fire on trespassers after three warnings.[19]

However, the much-dreaded Fenian rising never materialized. Far from triggering like incidents of violence, the Clerkenwell explosion cost the Fenians a good measure of whatever English sympathy there was, and public support evaporated overnight. In the wake of the December outrage many Irish communities publicly disavowed all connections with Fenianism, as at Swansea (Glamorgan):

> We hereby express our abhorrence of all armed violence, and all resistance to the civil power, being convinced that such measures are evil.... We cannot but disapprove of all secret societies, and especially of what is called 'The Fenian Brotherhood.'[20]

Even at Cleator Moor, a Cumberland mining town which harbored one of England's most pugnacious and aggressive Irish mobs, Fenianism disappeared. A leading Roman Catholic of Worcester wrote to *The Times* that there was not a single Irishman in that city who did not detest the Fenians. Even Bradlaugh severely denounced the "Clerkenwell outrage."[21]

The greatest embarrassment accrued to the Metropolitan Police and its aging superintendent, Sir Richard Mayne. The advance warning of the Clerkenwell explosion had been explicit. "It was so precise as to time, place, and *modus operandi* that the accomplishment of the plot ought to have been impossible," Derby wrote to Disraeli. "I am much inclined to think that Sir Richard Mayne is no longer equal to his post; from which, however, it would be very difficult to dismiss him, after so many years' service, without some flagrant proof of his incapacity." And again on the 17th: "It is really lamentable that the peace of the Metropolis...should depend on a body of police who, as detectives, are manifestly incompetent, and under a chief who, whatever may be his other merits, has not the energy, nor apparently, the skill to find out and employ men fitted for peculiar duties."[22] Hardy weakly tried to explain the police bungling in the House by saying that they thought the wall "would probably be blown up from underneath, and had no conception it would be blown down in the way it really was done."[23]

Though Hardy and Mayne were old friends, Hardy admitted that Mayne was inadequate to the Fenian challenge. He was aged and ailing, "wedded to the old ways." He would not cooperate with a rival detective system, and he was ineffective himself in following up the leads of other informants.[24] Hardy confided to Disraeli he "wishes to God he would resign." Disraeli agreed that nothing much could be done "if we don't get rid of Mayne," and urged Derby to insist upon this point.[25] Nevertheless, Mayne remained a year longer, until his death in December of the same year.

The search for detectives from among the Metropolitan force was notably unrewarding. Hardy believed that there was not a single man in the force who could be trusted with intelligence matters.[26] Instead, an experienced intelligence officer was found in the army, one W.H.A. Fielding, who was senior Army Intelligence Officer in Ireland.

Sir Richard Mayne

Police did manage to capture several of the Clerkenwell plotters, though not one of its masterminds, Captain Murphy. Burke, for his participation, was given an additional fifteen years, and one of the prime actors, a Michael Barrett, was convicted and sentenced to death by hanging. He was the last person to be publicly hanged in Britain.[27] The Queen was desperately anxious lest any should escape the full rigors of the law. She wrote to Hardy during the Fenian trials: "Seems dreadful that these people should escape. Indeed we begin to wish that these Fenians should be thought lynch-lawed and on the spot—as that would deter them far more than trials which continually break down...."[28]

Since the experience with Fenian terrorism was a new one to British police, the temptations to institute rather permanent mechanisms of suppression must have been great. That this was not done is a notable testimony to the Conservative dedication to the protection of civil rights even in these most threatening circumstances.

1. *The Times*, March 13, 1850.
2. See G. Kitson Clark, *The Making of Victorian England*, p. 77. At Glasgow and Dundee, the Irish accounted for 15.6% of the population. See also *The Times*, January 4, 1868.
3. See William D'Arcy, *The Fenian Movement in the United States* (1947).
4. HO 45 7799/759.
5. Russell to Wodehouse, January 25, February 14, 19, 1866; Russell Papers, P.R.O. 30/2216A/208.
6. HO 45/7799/171.
7. The story is most recently told in Leon O'Broin, *Fenian Fever: An Anglo-American Dilemma;* see also Annual Register (1867), II, 27; HO 45/7799/170–184.
8. HO 45/7799/165; Mayo to Disraeli, July 17, 1867, Hughenden Papers, B/XX/BO/37.
9. Cranbrook Papers, HA 43: T501/294, Diary for September 18, 1867; Hardy to Mayo, September 19, 1867, Mayo Papers, B.M. Add. Mss 11189/8; Lowe to Gladstone, November 29, 1873, BM Add. Mss 44302 f. 157–160.
10. Northcote to Hardy, October 2, 1867, quoted in Alfred E. Gathorne-Hardy, *Gathorne-Hardy, 1st Earl Cranbrook, A Memoir* (1920), I, p. 244.
11. HO 45/7799/287.
12. *3 Hansard* CXC (November 21, 1867), 114–129.
13. Gathorne-Hardy, 231–237.
14. The daily memos from the Home Office, P.R.O., HO 41/21–22; HO 45/7799/299 f.
15. *3 Hansard* CXC (March 9, 1867), 1215–1218.
16. Disraeli to Derby, December 16, 1867, Derby Papers, 146/3.

17. Derby to Disraeli, December 17, 1867, Hughenden Papers, B/XX/5/457.

18. Queen Victoria to Hardy, December 19, 1867, Cranbrook Papers, HA 43: T501/265.

19. HO 41/21/168ff; HO 45/799/289ff; *The Times*, January 2-8, 1868.

20. *Pall Mall Gazette*, January 2, 1868.

21. *The Times*, January 6, 1868; *National Reformer*, December 22, 1867.

22. Derby to Disraeli, December .15 and 17, 1867, Hughenden Papers, B/XX/5/456, 457.

23. *3 Hansard* CXC (March 9, 1868), 1218.

24. Hardy, I, pp. 217-227.

25. Disraeli to Derby, December 14, 1867, Derby Papers, 146/3.

26. Ibid., December 16, 1867.

27. Barrett's public hanging took place May 26, 1868, only three days before the Royal assent was given to the Capital Punishment Within Prisons Bill. For the story of public executions in England, see David M. Cooper, *The Lesson of the Scaffold* (1974).

28. Queen Victoria to Hardy, March 1, 1868, Cranbrook Papers, HA 43: T501/265,

3

WILLIAM MURPHY,
RABBLE-ROUSER

Apart from Fenianism there remained ample rancor between the Irish and the English that might erupt easily into violent hostility. One of the chief instigators of Catholic-Protestant confrontations were the Protestant lecturers and there were none more inflammatory than William Murphy.[1]

Murphy was born an Ulster Catholic, but while still a child his family secretly renounced Catholicism and lived for a time as closet Protestants. Upon exposure, the elder Murphy lost his teaching post and became a Protestant lecturer. William worked in a Dublin boot shop before joining his father on the lecture circuit. According to Murphy, his father was stoned to death during one of the inevitable collisions attending these lectures and Murphy fled to England. In the 1860s the Protestant Evangelical Mission and Electoral Union was sponsoring lecturers throughout the county and hired Murphy, who was then in his thirties.[2]

Murphy's provocative style pandered to the most emotional and excitable sentiments. Burning with vindictiveness and calumny, his lectures might more properly be described as tirades. "My name is Murphy, and a red hot one it is. I am for war with the knife, war with the revolver if you like, war with the bayonet if you like." Filled with the most abusive insults, his lectures were hardly calculated to convert anyone. He taunted Catholics in his audience with lurid fabrications of monastic lechery, of the seduction of young girls in the confessional, of priestly infanticide. "Your wives and your daughters are exposed to debauchery in the confessional, and are betrayed and kidnapped into convent prisons, and there kept the dupes or slaves of priestly lust."[3]

Murphy was not only abusive toward the Catholics, but also blatantly inflammatory. He told a Chelmsford (Essex) audience that "all the convents in England ought to be burnt," following which the local mob burned down the neighboring convent of New Hall. According to J.F. Maguire (M.P. for Cork) Murphy had publicly stated that Ireland could never be quiet till every Catholic priest was hanged.[4] And in Birmingham in 1867:

> Romanism was death; Protestantism was life.... Before he had finished his lectures he would prove to the people of Birmingham that every Popish priest was a murderer, a cannibal, a liar, and a pickpocket.... He was prepared to meet any Popish priest from Bishop Ullathorne to the biggest ragamuffin in the lot; and if ever there was a rag and bone gatherer in the universe it was the Pope himself....[5]

Murphy's platform style was both colorful and flamboyant. H.J. Hanham calls him "one of the greatest showmen of his age." A flier advertising a meeting in Lancashire read: "Protestants! Come and Hear the Questions put to the Married and the Unmarried in the Confessional, and Save your Wives and Family from Contamination."[6] The central feature of the evening's carefully orchestrated show was a simulation of a confessional in which Murphy and an accomplice mounted a mock confessional on the stage, and caricatured priest and confessor. Other Catholic ceremonies and sacraments were travestied, Catholic dogmas ridiculed, and Catholic leaders traduced as lecherous villains and worse.

The literature for sale at Murphy's meetings was similarly lurid and suspect. *Maria Monk,* an alleged account of the harrowing nightmare of an American nun, had been exposed long since as spurious. *The Confessional Unmasked,* an Electoral Union pamphlet, had been condemned as obscene by two English courts.[7] This work, dealing primarily with questions of sex and marriage, consisted of translations of Catholic authorities accompanied by derisive commentary.[8]

Not surprisingly, Murphy's circuses almost invariably provoked violent retaliation. His meetings were disrupted, he himself was assaulted, and his life was seriously threatened. At Beverly (Yorkshire) the local priest explained to city magistrates that many in his congregation "think no more of breaking Murphy's neck than they would of twisting the neck of a duck."[9] At Stonehouse (Glos) a large band of Irish forcibly closed his meetings. A mob at Frome (Somerset) threatened hanging. During a "lecture" on the doctrine of infallibility at Plymouth (Devon), Murphy found himself under attack by 150 Irish men and women, some armed with shillelaghs. A band of marines rescued Murphy and escorted him home.[10]

In the certain expectation of tumult, apprehensive local authorities worried over the best means of preserving the public peace without infringing upon the right of public assembly, the classic dilemma. In July, 1865, the magistrates of Chelmsford (Essex) on their own authority simply refused Murphy the use of a hall. Others, however grudgingly, tolerated his presence and took steps to prevent the outbreak of hostilities. At Wolverhampton (Stafford) in February, 1867, a series of meetings commenced with such violence that the mayor personally requested Murphy to desist. Upon Murphy's adamant refusal, the mayor swore in special constables and borrowed county forces, explaining to the Home Office: "The magistrates are unwilling themselves to stop the Lecture as it seems a direct interference with the right to meet and discuss any question." The magistrates appealed to the better judgment of the townspeople in a public notice:

> The Magistrates have been advised that they have no power legally to stop the lecture of Mr. Murphy tonight. Notwithstanding they are of opinion that the placards issued by him respecting that Lecture are most offensive to a large body of the Inhabitants. The Magistrates are taking effective measures to preserve the Peace, but they call upon the Inhabitants not to countenance by their presence, in the Streets or elsewhere, any assembly by which the Peace of the Town is endangered. John Morris, Mayor.[11]

With special constables and troops from Coventry and Birmingham, the remaining meetings passed off without incident and Walpole expressed approval of the course followed, though allowing himself the admission "Murphy is a perfect nuisance."[12]

During the tumultuous reform agitation of the summer of 1867 Murphy opposed any enlarged franchise for Ireland on the ground that it would only augment the Catholic danger. In June, at the height of the Reform League demonstrations, he planned a series of political meetings in Birmingham lasting five weeks.[13] The mayor denied Murphy use of the spacious Town Hall and he was forced to resort to the portable "tabernacle" he had used many times already. Even before the meetings began, the wooden structure was vandalized and on the evening prior to the opening lecture, the entire roof was pulled off. On opening night there occurred the predictable anti-Murphy riot[14] followed by a Protestant storming of the Irish quarter of Birmingham. Large sections of the area were left actually gutted.[15] Joseph Chamberlain recalled, "I went down next day to see the place; the roofs were gone; the fronts of the houses also; the remains of the fires were still to be seen."[16] By the 18th the magistrates had marshalled 93 cavalry, three hundred infantry (including one hundred pensioners) and about 580 policemen besides four or five hundred special constables, but the situation remained precarious. The mayor wrote to the Home Secretary (Gathorne-Hardy):

> ...Mr. Murphy used language last night, indicating an opinion that it would be serviceable if the mayor got a couple more blows....the priests of Rome were murderers, cannibals, pickpockets, and liars— and that it was his intention to remain five weeks longer in Birmingham....It has therefore occurred to the magistrates to ask your advice under these difficult circumstances. We are advised that there are grounds for believing that Murphy has transgressed the laws—and certainly his presence endangers the peace of the Town. I should be glad if you would suggest some course for us to take....

Hardy privately asked for Waddington's advice and was confirmed in his uncomfortable realization that there was no process of law by which a man such as Murphy could be prevented from lecturing unless he could be brought under indictment for inciting to a breach of the peace.[17] The Conservative Home Office was also sensitive to the dangers of being drawn into the affair in a way that might be construed as interfering with the rights of assembly and free speech. Hardy allowed himself only the frustrated comment that Murphy's language was "most unjustifiable."

The press decried the disturbances as "Murphy riots," and unanimously attributed their cause to the firebrand orator. But in Commons the following summer, Murphy's defenders charged that the Irish had instigated the fights. "Mr. Murphy had played the part of a lamb, and the wolfish proceedings of the other side were not his fault," claimed Whalley, an arch-critic of Catholicism.[18] While it is difficult to visualize Murphy as a lamb, it seems evident that neither the Irish nor the Murphyites shirked from the confrontation.

From Birmingham, Murphy set out for the smaller manufacturing districts of Lancashire where the cotton famine had already created the hard times especially conducive to disturbances.[19]

> I am going to Ashton to lecture in a cotton mill, and within 300 to 400 yards of the Catholic Chapel, and it will not take us long to drive the Popish lambs to Paddy's land. If the people once break out in Lancashire, they will first seize the Catholic priests, then the Sisters of Mercy, and afterwards the lambs, and send them all afloat, neck and crop.[20]

It was here in Lancashire that Murphy found the most combustible material for his inflammatory message. Riots broke out spontaneously wherever he lectured and frequently persisted long after he was gone. In some towns the mere announcement of his coming was sufficient to send the Irish into a frenzy. The more serious of these riots occurred at Ashton, Oldham, Rochdale, Bury, Blackburn, and Bacup; in Staffordshire at Stone and Hanley; in Cheshire at Staleybridge. At Bacup, Murphy's party paraded through the Irish section of town behind a man bearing a naked sword.[21]

The Home Office received a steady stream of complaints from Murphy and other Protestant lecturers claiming lack of adequate police protection. One such letter from Murphy (March, 1868):

> Sir—I beg leave to inform you that a murderous assualt was made upon me and my colleague Mr. Geo. Mackey, on Monday night last, about eight o'clock in the town of Rochdale....The heading of the placard 'Popery and Puseyism' seems to have caused the mayor *half an hour* before we arrived in the town to have the directors (of the hall we had taken) together and got them to put up a placard stating that the hall would be closed in consequence of an anticipated riot if the lectures were allowed to be delivered. Now Sir we got no intimation of this until we arrived and found ourselves surrounded by a hostile mob thirsting for our blood. And no adequate force at the hall—only *three or four* policemen....The few police were powerless and we had a very narrow escape for our lives—A few wounds in the face and some blows on the body with a mile's race in a cab off which the missiles hopped like hailstones,...We are determined to have our lectures which are perfectly legal delivered in Rochdale. We will die rather than resign our rights and surely the authorities will not allow a Popish mob to deprive a man of liberty of speech....[22]

The lecturer wished Hardy to telegraph the mayor of Rochdale to order extra protection, but Hardy merely replied that he had no doubts that the Rochdale authorities would proceed properly. Murphy himself wrote to the Home Office a week later:

> Sir, Being about to visit Rochdale in My Capasity [sic] of Protestant
> lecturer for the Evangelical Mission of London, and My life so often
> been threatened both by letter and open violance [sic] and doubting
> my being able to obtain that protection from the authorities of the
> above town which is due to all her Magesty's [sic] loyal subjects
> from Mob Law and Fenian Asassenation [sic]. I am a loyal and faithful
> subject...and as such I am entitled to all the protection the State can
> give me. I therefore beg you will issue such an order to those in author-
> ity in Rochdale as will compel them to grant the protection and not
> for them to interfere with my rights and liberties as an Englishman so
> long as I do not transgress the Law—but if the law denies me protection
> from the violance [sic] my life is threatened with I shall then be
> obliged to protect myself as best I can....
>
> I again beg Sir you will issue your order for My protection not only in
> Rochdale but in all other towns I hope to visit. I have the Honor to
> remain your obedient and Humble Servant, William Murphy.[23]

The Conservative Home Office refused to be drawn into the
affair on the side of the Protestant lecturers. Hardy succinctly
ordered that Murphy be advised to apply routinely to local magistrates: "They will no doubt take proper steps to prevent any
breach of the peace." On the 17th a telegram arrived from
Murphy: "According to your orders I have applied for protection
and am told by Mr. Thomas Bright that he would rather imprison
than protect me..."[24] But the mayor, several days later, did call
for a troop of Hussars who remained for a while in Rochdale, and
no rioting occurred on this occasion. Somewhat more candidly
Hardy wrote to Lord Denbigh: "All that the Law justifies shall be
done on my part to put down such violence which brings disgrace
upon the name of religion with which it is spuriously associated....
I am not surprised at your indignation but I have to look to legal
measures and consequences."[25] After another similar telegram
from Murphy and an opposing letter from the magistrates at
Bacup, the exasperated Hardy penned in the margin: "Murphy is
a positive nuisance and I think ought if possible to be stopped."[26]
How to accomplish that aim remained an enigma.

By far the most bloody and destructive of the Lancashire riots
were those of May 9–11 at Ashton–under–Lyne. The Protestant
Electoral Union sponsored a "tea party" May 9, at which conspicuous orange emblems and ribbons were distributed. The next
day, Sunday, the English Protestants thronged the streets flaunting
their orange ribbons and the Irish their green. The inevitable heckling quickly escalated to open rioting which raged uncontrolled for

several hours. Since Murphy was not yet present, the police were taken entirely by surprise. The Irish got the worst of the battle and later charged that the magistrates did nothing to quell the rioting for four hours. Later the same evening, the Protestant mob surged into the Irish quarter of Ashton, and amid general street fighting, demolished most of the houses in several streets, damaged two Catholic Chapels and one school, and smashed innumerable windows elsewhere. At a later hour county police forces reinforced by special constables restored a shaky peace.

Monday morning the disturbances broke out again and continued throughout the day. About seven o'clock in the evening the Protestants massed in a poor ˜ection of the Irish quarter, Reyner Row, and began again to sack one house after another.

> The rioters met with little or no opposition and in a very short time every house in the row was forcibly entered, the window frames and doors were smashed to atoms, and the furniture and bedding were hurled into the street, where they were burnt. Tables, chairs, sofas, pictures,...ornaments, carpets—all were thrown into one heterogeneous mass and consumed by flames.[27]

The Home Office was irritated by an apparent lack of communication from local authorities. Hardy complained to Disraeli: "Though we telegraphed more than once yesterday [May 11] no written communication has come from that place. I had ordered a letter to be written requesting full details and if the magistrates do not give a satisfactory account I think that I shall send someone to inquire on the spot."[28] Troops easily routed concentrated groups of rioters, but they fled from one street only to re-form in another and resume their destructive spree. In the melee a sixty-seven-year-old woman was trampled to death.

For several days the Protestant armed mob ransacked the Irish sectors of Ashton, demolishing two chapels, one hall, one school, and over 110 houses and shops. Several Irish suffered severe physical brutalities but only one victim died. Maguire moved for an immediate Parliamentary investigation, but unsuccessfully. Some of the more openly anti-Catholic English Members placed the blame squarely on the Irish-Catholics.

As in the previous year, the press identified Murphy and the Protestant Electoral Union lecturers as instigators of the riots. The *Manchester Guardian* was openly antagonistic:

It is unhappily a mere matter of fact that if certain incitements are used and certain passions appealed to, we may see aroused in...many more English towns the hatreds which have just wrecked 110 houses and two chapels in Ashton-under-Lynn....Set the Protestant Electoral Union with its Murphys to work, and you will excite these storms as certainly as a spark will raise a fire in straw....These "lectures" convince no one, and they are certain, in such towns as Ashton and Birmingham, to give rise to a kind of civil war.[29]

The same week in which the *Guardian's* editorial appeared, Murphy-Irish riots broke out in other towns of southern Lancashire. On Monday evening, May 25, an English mob attacked a Roman Catholic church at Oldham and shattered all its windows. On Tuesday evening the rioters pelted the police with rocks because they were guarding the Catholic church there. At midnight the same night, a band of Irish from Oldham marched to nearby Hollinwood and, appearing entirely unexpectedly, destroyed without opposition most of the windows of the Baptist church and the Unitarian chapel. On Wednesday, May 27, Oldham magistrates urged all citizens to stay at home and swore in one hundred special constables. This time Oldham's Protestant mob took to the road and hiked to Failsworth where, at 9:00 P.M., they smashed every pane of glass in that community's Catholic chapel. By Thursday evening, groups of townsmen stationed themselves in front of most churches and chapels in the area to protect them from the roving gangs. In spite of them, an Irish mob of 150 succeeded in one last stroke of revenge. Armed with bludgeons, they marched four abreast to Harpurhey and stoned an Independent chapel; they then trooped to Miles Platting and damaged St. John's Church.

During the summer the *Manchester Guardian* continued its campaign against Murphy's lectures recommending that the authorities prevent them because "he has only to announce his intention of visiting any place, and the whole population is thrown into alarm."[30] By July the official neutrality of the Home Office began to waver. In response to the alarmed authorities of Bolton, where Murphy threatened to visit, Liddell telegraphed the following advice:

If Mr. Murphy proposes to deliver his lectures in a private room the Magistrates have no power to prevent him. If he proposes to do so in the street or in a public place within their jurisdiction, the Magistrates

having had information on oath laid before them that the delivery of
such lecture was likely to lead to a breach of the peace, should give
Mr. Murphy notice that he will not be allowed to lecture in such
public place, and should take all necessary steps to prevent him doing
so.[31]

Murphy then announced he would seek election to Parliament on
a Protestant platform and called for an open air meeting for
September 5 at 5:00 P.M. in Chorlton Road on the outskirts of
Manchester. By 4:00 P.M. a dense crowd had already gathered and
was listening to one of Murphy's colleagues when an Irish mob
approached and surrounded the meeting site. With five to six
thousand persons present, the police were helpless to prevent a
collision, and before city reinforcements arrived, a fierce fight had
spilled over into the heavily populated streets of the city. By the
time Murphy appeared on the scene at 5:00 P.M., the Irish had been
driven away and the Orangemen greeted their man with wild
cheers, three groans for Popery, and the National Anthem. That
day and the next, when smaller riots threatened, the police
arrested a total of forty-two persons, mostly Irish.

During 1869 opposition to Murphy grew on the part of both
the magistrates and the Irish. Murphy went to Northumberland in
March and began a series of lectures at the Odd Fellows' Hall at
Tynemouth. On Friday, the 19th, a well-organized band of Irishmen numbering two to four hundred from Jarrow, Walker, Wellington Quay, and other nearby towns marched in military fashion
to the meeting chanting, "We'll kill Murphy." Alerted beforehand,
a large body of police guarded the hall but were unable to prevent
the attackers from firing shots into the building and shattering all
the windows. Some of the English escaped by a rear door, but
Murphy and most of his followers hurriedly converted the stage
into an improvised fort and, armed with chair legs, prepared to
defend themselves against the invaders. However, in a bloody
battle outside, the police succeeded in dispersing the Irish
assailants, and the Murphyites escaped harm.[32]

Following the Liberal victory of 1868, Henry Austin Bruce
replaced Hardy at the Home Office. He was a Welsh coal owner,
barrister, and history buff. Like most educated Victorians he knew
Greek and Latin, in grammar school committing the earlier books
of the *Iliad* to memory and reciting the lesson with his book

upside down. He proceeded not to Oxford or Cambridge, but to Lincoln's Inn and was called to the bar at the age of twenty-two. Quitting the bar scarcely five years later he explained, "I am tired of pursuing a career for which I have no calling, tired of the hypocrisy of pretending to work,...tired, in short, of being a useless member of society....London is not destined to be the scene of my greatness or my usefulness." He proposed to "...lounge through life. For this is all I am fit for." After several years in southern Italy he returned to Wales, became police magistrate of Merthyr Tydfil, and announced, "Nothing could have happened more fortunately for me. The absolute necessity of attending to my duties has supplied me with a motive to order and regularity, which I never should have found in my own nature. I am virtuous on compulsion." Nevertheless, in 1848 he yet considered himself "a lazy, discursive, purposeless wretch."[33] By 1852 he had entered Commons as Member for Merthyr and served for two years as Under Secretary at the Home Office under Grey (1862-1864). It was again Grey to whom Gladstone turned in 1868, and only upon Grey's refusal at another stint (he had run that course three times) did Gladstone invite Bruce to the Home Office.[34] Bruce, at that point, did not even have a seat in Commons, having lost at Merthyr in 1868, but as frequently occurred in the nineteenth century, he accepted the post and then sought a seat, finding one the following month at Renfrewshire.

Bruce's copious letters and speeches reveal a humane and conscientious man concerned with social issues, but cautious about reforms and wary of revolution. A staunch Anglican, he devoted most of his public speaking to exhortations in favor of adult education and against "brutalizing drunkenness." His Licensing Act regulating the public houses, even in its much diluted form as passed, was said to have driven every English brewer into the Conservative party. For the working classes Bruce prescribed the cultivation of book-reading, "the only counterpoise to the beer house."[35]

Bruce abandoned even the pretense of neutrality in the controversy over Murphy, a man he considered a simple troublemaker. In April of 1869 he asked the Law Officers to suggest a statute by which Murphy's meetings might lawfully be stopped. Collier and Coleridge disinterred an act passed originally in 1799

Henry Bruce, Lord Aberdare

to deal with the French Catholic threat, the Act for Suppression of Seditious and Treasonable Practices.[36] On this legal base, and since the Tynemouth episode had been perilously close to a fatal conflict, the Home Office let it be known that such meetings could be prohibited. Magistrates throughout Northumberland then refused to grant Murphy facilities for meetings, and when he returned to Tynemouth for further meetings in April, the mayor upon direct advice from the Home Office proscribed the meetings and threatened a fine of £20 on all who attended. At North Shields the mayor served notice on the proprietor of the building Murphy had hired to not allow the meeting.

In Commons, Bruce defended his posture on pragmatic grounds: "Here is a man, who for no good purpose whatever, goes about exciting the peaceful inhabitants of towns in such a way as to lead to violence,...and as long as there are means of repression known to the law, I think it is the duty of those charged with the preservation of the peace to use them."[37] Murphy, outraged, of course, both by the speech and by the Government's policies, wrote to Bruce again in the guise of a loyal and humble citizen:

> ...I lecture for useful purpose and in a lawful manner and even if I only lecture for my living, I deserve protection in so doing....Yet it appears that under an obsolete or torpid Act of Parliament the Magistrates have under the direction of the Home Office, closed any Hall and have threatened me with penalty of £100, and any person who may attend my lectures with a penalty of £20....And this is the whole question; they who don't like me declare that if I am allowed to lecture *they will create riots.* There is then no law but that of violence which has too often been suffered by me and my friends, but violence never has been begun nor provoked on our part. The Irish mob so gallantly put to flight by the local police came to Shields crying 'we will kill Murphy if we are hung for it.'

> As an Irishman I admit the excitable temperament of my race and the greatest zeal in the cause I have undertaken; but as long as no evidence can be brought against me of using 'language apt to cause a breach of the peace,' except insofar as illconditioned persons commit a breach of the peace when they hear what they don't like, which is tyranny, I claim full protection against violence on the one side and full liberty to pursue without molestation either by Irish mobs or officers of the peace.

> I do not go to Irishmen and provoke their prejudices, I desire to get Halls furthest from them. They come to me, I do not go to them. Not only do they come to my meetings but they day by day and hour by hour, watch about my home, if I open my window they spit in my face

again and again, young girls direct from the Roman Catholic schools
assail myself and wife with obscene language most gross and disgusting
and almost beyond the most depraved minds to imagine.[38]

Murphy, in similar earnest language, demanded a personal interview with Bruce which was denied.

When Murphy returned to Birmingham later in June the mayor
concluded that no police force available could prevent riot and
therefore ordered Murphy's arrest: "...Believing that I can find a
justification of my conduct in Moral law, I seek it not in Statute
law. If I have done Mr. Murphy any wrong I am willing that a
jury should assess the damage."[39] He explained to Bruce, "you
will perceive that I consulted nothing but necessity." Murphy
was held in jail overnight and all charges dismissed in the morning.
In this case Bruce admitted doubtful legality of the course pursued, but assumed that the mayor had acted on the principle
salus populi suprema lex.[40] Murphy and his followers quite
naturally denounced all such techniques of repression, and charged
Catholic priests with instigating opposition by certifying to
magistrates that riots would ensue if his meetings were allowed.
"And to this intimidation, the dastardly, unjust magistrates yield.
A mob forbids Murphy lecturing; and with infamous pusillanimity,
the magistrates administer that mob law."[41]

Having lived all his life amid scenes of hatred and violence,
William Murphy died from injuries sustained at the hands of an
angry Irish mob in Cumberland. Threatening crowds had attacked
him on innumerable occasions, yet he never desisted. The incident
which took his life occurred at the Odd Fellows' Hall of the tiny
coastal town of Whitehaven where he began a series of talks in
April, 1871. On Sunday the 20th, a mob of Irish miners from the
town of Cleator Moor, three or four miles distant, arrived by train
in Whitehaven with concealed weapons of every description. One
miner brought along his crowbar. Inconspicuously the miners
strolled into the hall about an hour before the meeting was to
begin and found Murphy alone in an anteroom. Instantly they
rushed him, threw him over a bannister and down a flight of stairs;
at the foot of the stairs they mauled him till he lay unconscious.
The mob continued to kick and strike him until police at last
broke through and dragged him away. At the trial in April, Super-

intendent Little described the scene at the Odd Fellows' Hall just after the Irish "delegation" entered:

> Immediately we heard a yell, a cry out 'They are murdering Murphy!' We immediately repaired to the entrance door. They were all in a crowd, and appeared as if they had got some person under their feet. When we got to the spot, I saw Mr. Murphy on the ground, face downwards, bleeding very much, and these parties round about him.... I thought that the man was killed outright.[42]

While Murphy lay dying in a hospital, seven of his attackers received from three to twelve months imprisonment.[43] By the time Murphy finally succumbed in March, 1872, his attackers had almost completed their terms of imprisonment. Birmingham surgeons conducted a post mortem and declared that the cause of death was directly traceable to Murphy's Whitehaven injuries. Even in death Murphy inspired violence, and his funeral on March 18, in Birmingham, was attended by disorderly scenes and brick-throwing along the procession route.[44]

The Murphy riots (more accurately anti-Murphy riots) serve as another reminder of the intense Victorian commitments *both* to freedom of speech *and* the demands of public order. The head-on collision of these mutually-competing principles could only remain an unresolved dilemma. Under certain circumstances the balance might tilt one way or the other, and partisans might exaggerate the violation of their own positions, but most mid-Victorians condemned Murphy for creating the dilemma in the first place. Whatever protection he did receive from authorities was provided most grudgingly. When he was dead, the public tried to forget him as quickly as possible.

1. The Home Office files on Murphy are found in P.R.O. HO 41/7991.

2. *The Times*, May 29, 1868; 3 *Hansard* CXCII (1868), 1090.

3. *The Times*, May 28, 1868.

4. 3 *Hansard* CXCII (1868), 830, 820.

5. *Annual Register* (1867), II, 79. Bishop Ullathorne was the Roman Catholic Bishop of Birmingham.

6. H.J. Hanham, *Elections and Party Management: Politics In the Age of Disraeli and Gladstone*, pp. 305–306.

7. 3 *Hansard* CXCII (1868), 820.

8. Protestant Evangelical Mission and Electoral Union, *Report of the Trial of Mr. George Mackey, Containing the Full Text of the Morality of Romish Devotion or The Confessional Unmasked.*

9. *3 Hansard* CCXI (1872), 965, 966.

10. *The Times*, June 8, 1866; *3 Hansard* CCXI (1872), 966.

11. Mayor of Wolverhampton to Home Office, February 21, 1867, and Public Notice, February 22, 1867.

12. P.R.O. HO 45/7991/1-63.

13. *Annual Register* (1867), II, 79; Dona Torr, *Tom Mann and His Times* (1948), I, 42.

14. *3 Hansard* CXCII (1868), 1089; *Annual Register* (1867), II, 79. Police arrested twenty-six rioters.

15. Hanham, 305.

16. James Garvin, *Life of Joseph Chamberlain*, I, p. 90.

17. Mayor of Birmingham to Hardy, June 18, 1867, P.R.O. HO 45/7991/10; Waddington to Mayor of Birmingham, June 19, 1867, HO 41/20/340.

18. *3 Hansard* CXCII (1868), 1090.

19. Hanham, p. 306.

20. *The Times*, May 28, 1868.

21. Hanham, p. 306; *The Times*, May 29, 1868; *Sunderland Herald*, March 20, 1868.

22. James Houston to Home Office, March 4, 1868; HO 45/7991/19. Houston was employed by the Evangelical Mission.

23. William Murphy to Home Office, March 13, 1868, HO 45/7991/21.

24. Telegram, Murphy to Home Office, March 17, 1868, HO 45/7991/22.

25. Hardy to Denbigh, April 14, 1868, HO 45/7991/26.

26. HO 45/7991/30.

27. *Annual Register* (1868), II, 55; *3 Hansard* CXCII (1868), 818-827.

28. Hardy to Disraeli, May 12, 1868; Hughendon Papers B/XX/Ha/30.

29. *Manchester Guardian*, May 27, 1868.

30. Ibid., June 4, 1868.

31. HO 45/7991/58.

32. *3 Hansard* CXCII (1868), 615; *Annual Register* (1869), II, 22.

33. *Letters of the Rt. Hon. Henry Austin Bruce* (1902), privately printed, Vol. I, p. 43, 51, 87 ff.

34. Gladstone Papers, BM Add. Mss. 44162 f 309-312.

35. H.A. Bruce, *Letters and Addresses*, p. 62 ff.

36. Geo III c. 79 s15 as qualified by 9 & 10 Vict c 33.

37. *3 Hansard* CVC (1869), 759-60.

38. Murphy to Bruce, April 20, 1869, HO 45/7991/61.

39. Mayor of Birmingham to Home Office, June 19, 1869, HO 45/7991/63.

40. *3 Hansard* CVC (1869), 411.

41. Protestant Evangelical Mission and Electoral Union, *Report of the Trial of Mr. George Mackey, Containing the Full Text of the Morality of Romish Devotion or The Confessional Unmasked*, p. iii.

42. *Whitehaven Herald*, April 29, 1871.

43. *3 Hansard* CCXI (1872), 949.

44. *Manchester Guardian*, March 19, 1872.

4

THE STRUGGLE FOR HYDE PARK

I t seems difficult to overemphasize how much the British people have cherished (or believe they have cherished) certain civil rights throughout their history, and most particularly the right of free speech and public meeting. Speaker's Corner in the shadow of Marble Arch has become a modern Mars Hill, a green symbol of a traditional freedom. But the right of public meeting, even in Hyde Park, was not unchallenged until the latter half of the nineteenth century, and then only after countless determined confrontations, both legal and physical. A study of the Hyde Park encounters of the 1860s provides a clearer understanding of the working of the Victorian Home Office, police, and military in the face of massed demonstrators.

If it had been possible, the Superintendent of the Metropolitan Police since its inception, Sir Richard Mayne, would have tolerated no public speaking in Hyde Park whatsoever. His most notorious ban was issued during the summer of 1855 in connection with opposition to Lord Grosvenor's Sunday closing bill.[1] In defiance of the ban, which had the blessing of Sir George Grey, Sunday gatherings in the park grew more ominous and tumultuous through June and July until Lord Grosvenor suddenly withdrew his bill. It was at one of these Sunday demonstrations that Charles Bradlaugh experienced for the first time the exhilaration of a face-to-face defiance of police. The policeman backed away. Bradlaugh himself later recalled this incident as "a first step in a course in which I have never flinched or wavered."[2] Again in 1862 Sir Richard Mayne proscribed by placards all Sunday meetings in the parks, the occasion being popular support for Garibaldi. Banned were all "meetings for the purpose of delivereing or hearing speeches, or for the public discussion of popular and exciting topics," phraseology utilized until 1870.[3]

Of all the agitations of the eighteen-sixties none burgeoned so threateningly as that of the franchise reformers. Though Parliament had rejected bills in 1852, 1854, 1859, and 1860, the reaction of the populace remained apathetic, a source of the greatest dismay to the reformers. But within several months of the death of Palmerston, reform of the franchise suddenly came to the fore as one of Hugo's ideas whose time had come again. Reform demonstrations became the rage, Edmund Beales' Reform League in the vanguard.[4]

There followed in quick succession a series of spectacular bank failures culminating in Black Friday (May 11, 1866), Commons' rejection of another of Lord Russell's Reform Bills, his resignation in mid-June, the announcement of the proposed Derby cabinet, and a mammoth protest rally scheduled for July 2.[5] Sir Richard impulsively ordered a ban then withdrew it: a crowd of thirty to sixty thousand turned out. Gathering courage, Beales excitedly called for an even bigger demonstration three weeks later (July 23). Confronted with prospects of a potentially explosive gathering, a tired Sir Richard sought advice from the Home Office. The new Home Secretary in Derby's third ministry was Spencer Walpole (see Chapter II) who had just taken the office a week earlier. Walpole and Mayne decided to post a ban on the Hyde Park meeting of July 23, a decision whose consequences were destined to cost both men far more than either could have been expected to foresee.

The League argued more and more divisively as the date for the confrontation approached. On July 20 Beales outlined the League's options in a final strategy meeting. W. R. Cremer advised compliance with the ban, and Charles Bradlaugh, by then already one of the country's outstanding "public lecturers," urged total defiance. The result was the well-known compromise whereby the League, while not cancelling the meeting, would only formally demand access to the park, and upon refusal, retreat to Trafalgar Square.[6] Sir Richard realized immediately that any such scenario acted out in the midst of thousands of excited and perhaps armed demonstrators had little chance of avoiding serious disorder. But bolstered by a sympathetic Home Office the Superintendent resolved not to cancel his prohibition for Monday, July 23.

The day of the showdown dawned sunny in London; the temperature was unseasonably high. In the early afternoon young John Hardy, son of Walpole's second in command, strolled through the park and noticed a "great lot of roughs about."[7] By early evening from 1600 to 1800 constables ringed the park, concentrated at the entrances. Walpole had already requested "as a measure of protection" that troops in the metropolis be held in readiness and that the senior officers be formally empowered to comply with any police call without further resort to the Secretary. No costly delays were to be risked due to formalities in the chain of command.[8]

By 7:00 P.M., when Beales and the committee arrived at Marble Arch, huge crowds already swirled around the square. Alighting from their cabs amidst some inevitable pushing and shoving, Beales and the committee succeeded in being more or less formally turned away at the entrance. Bradlaugh later charged police roughness: "V.32 backing his horse right on Beales and myself. The trunchcons were all out."[9] Beales and some others then departed in the cabs for Trafalgar Square, while Bradlaugh and other League lieutenants attempted to siphon the crowds in the same direction. The handbills they distributed urging departure for Trafalgar Square were trampled underfoot unread. While Beales was commencing a small orderly meeting at Nelson's Column, the congestion and tumult outside the park increased. Excited to fever pitch by the banners and the temperature, the milling crowd pressed ever more insistently against the iron railings separating them from the open spaces and flower beds of Hyde Park. An eyewitness from Park Lane across from the park described the scene as the railings went down:

> The barriers down, a vast body of men poured through the breaches, many injuries were received, and the police, hearing of the occurrence, came tumbling up from the main gate and charged the struggling mass with drawn truncheons. They might as well have charged the Falls of Niagara. Mrs. Partington confronting the Atlantic with her broom was not a more ludicrous picture. They belaboured the front ranks with their batons, but were swept aside like flies before the waiter's napkin.[10]

As soon as the railings were breached, Mayne called in the military to reinforce the police. Fifty soldiers rushed to defend Marble Arch; a regiment of Life Guards was sent to patrol New Ride to prevent the use of its stones against the police; five com-

panies of Coldstream Guards were deployed strategically at the
park entrances. Nevertheless, it proved impossible to prevent the
exhilarated crowds, who were cheering even the military, from
milling through the park. Clearance was not effected before midnight.[11] A testimony to Victorian restraint, the greatest injury
was sustained not by individuals, but by the park's flower beds.
And although the younger Hardy found them the next afternoon
in "a very much damaged state," a former Commissioner of
Works, a Mr. Cowper, recalled that "even in the heat and hurry
of the disturbance" he saw demonstrators who "went round along
the grass so as not to tread upon the flower-beds and borders."[12]

But for the next three days the crowds were back. On Tuesday
the windows of the Athenaeum and the United Service Clubs were
stoned, perhaps the result of a noticeable increase in the proportion of idlers and ruffians in the mob. Once again the police
proved unable to corral the roving crowds, and by late afternoon
the Guards were called in again to effect clearance. Even before
Paulet arrived at 5:00, Mayne had already called in the Second
Life Guards to the Serpentine. By 9:00 the crowds had so increased in numbers that Mayne ordered troop reinforcements
again, and Paulet brought the Coldstream Guards from Knightsbridge to the Magazine and the battery at Chelsea was moved to
Knightsbridge. At dusk, it was decided to use force once more to
eject the crowds. The remaining Life Guards and the Coldstream
Guards from the Magazine were paraded into the park as a gesture
of support for the police, and the latter then charged the crowd
which dispersed without further resistance. In half an hour the park
was cleared save for stragglers.[13] As the troops returned to their
barracks Walpole, a few miles away, was defending his actions in
the House, with what Hardy thought was indisputable vindica-
tion.[14]

On Wednesday the promise of yet another ugly confrontation
stirred fears in both camps. Walpole felt overwhelmed by the unexpected consequences of his actions and sent an urgent request
to the Law Officers for an interpretation of the Law Officer's
Opinion of 1856 in the present circumstances, with special attention to the legality of ejecting crowds already in the park.[15]
During the next five days he called up the Royal Horse Guards

from Aldershot to quarters inside Hyde Park, Regent's Park, and the Royal Mews in Pimlico.

On Wednesday the League was having its own misgivings. The League had always prided itself on the self-discipline of its rallies. Now the growing number of frivolous elements, the riot-for-the-fun-of-it types, might bring the whole movement into disrepute. These and other considerations led the League to send Beales at the head of a delegation to the Home Office with an offer to restore order in Hyde Park on condition that all troops and police be removed from the park. A grateful Walpole accepted immediately, with such a sense of relief that it was said he wept.[16]

These agreements were made on Wednesday, July 25. On the same day Hardy, walking in the park, met Walpole and Disraeli, and Walpole told him that he had a "guarantee from the League people to withdraw the mob," a proceeding which struck Hardy as a "very doubtful bargain—responsibility with non-responsibility." Gossip was that the League had extracted in return a promise from Walpole that it might be allowed to hold its meeting in Hyde Park the following Monday at 6:00, rumors that Hardy could not believe: "It would indeed be an abdication of its functions by the Executive."[17] Hardy was not the only one concerned. Derby wrote on Thursday to Disraeli: "I am very anxious to see you about this fiasco of Walpole's.... The matter is serious and pressing."[18]

The Cabinet held a special session on the park affair on Friday, after which explanations were tendered in both Houses. Another longer Cabinet session was held on Saturday. It was on Saturday that the Law Officers rendered their opinion. While allowing the legality of the initial ban on political meetings in Hyde Park, Cairns and Bovill advised that it would be "impractical" to attempt clearance of any great number of demonstrators. "...In our Opinion there is not for any practical Purpose a legal Authority to disperse by Force a Meeting of the kind supposed, consisting of a large number of persons, and that whether Notice has or has not been given."[19] The Law Opinion furnished little comfort to Walpole, who could now only hope the League would not persist in its challenge: "It is very difficult to deal with a refuse population coming merely for riot." Under the circumstances it is not surprising that Walpole appeared bewildered. Hardy wrote that during the long Cabinet meeting on Saturday the Home Secretary "was not decisive and seemed confused, but he is over-worked in all ways."[20] At the logical urging of J.S. Mill the League temporarily abandoned its Hyde Park claims.

There was some uneasiness with respect to the stragglers and roughs who lingered for some evenings in the park. Gladstone referred to them as "the scum of the people" and made no mention of them in Commons "because I think undue and factitious importance may be given thereby."[21] But by the end of the week even these elements were persuaded by the League to leave, and Beales could claim to have saved all London from "most disastrous scenes of violence and bloodshed."[22]

The Government's park problem was only shelved, not solved. Large crowds continued to turn out for reform demonstrations throughout the country. Bright attracted 100,000 at Birmingham in August and filled Manchester's Free Trade Hall the following month. In Leeds a mammoth workingman's reform procession stretched for four miles. October meetings in Glasgow and Edinburgh drew thirty thousand and fifty thousand, respectively.[23] In spite of the high numbers involved, the giant autumn meetings and processions were notable for a high degree of self-policing and an absence of serious disorder. Organizers had accepted to a certain extent an obligation for controlling the crowds they were responsible for attracting. The League routinely appointed marshalls, sometimes mounted, to keep order at demonstrations. Bradlaugh was most energetic during these days in this capacity, creating something of a legend on his little brown horse.[24]

Nevertheless, memories of the trampled Hyde Park flower beds lingered, and the Government found itself under severe pressure to deal more stringently with mammoth demonstrations in the aftermath of July 23. One illustration may suffice: Lord Ellenborough, frightened at the disorderly prospects of an announced demonstration in Trafalgar Square of the Trades' Societies on December 3, advised Derby to take extreme precautions. He urged secret nocturnal rushing of troops to London, a great show of military strength to overawe the demonstrators. "Some of these precautions may be deemed superfluous, but it was the lack of previous preparations that mainly led to the capture of the Tuileries in 1838 [1848] and thereby to the fall of the French Monarchy. There can be no mistake about the meaning of this measure of the 3rd of December. It means Revolution and nothing less, and under the circumstances that object would be accompanied by the sacking of London. It must be met accordingly."[25] But there is no indication that Derby attempted any influence over the Home Office, and although Walpole did call in the 14th Hussars from Hounslow for standby on December 3, there was no need for their intervention.[26] The Trades' Societies furnished ten thousand volunteer Keepers of the Peace from their own ranks, and these beribboned forces enabled the police to remain in the background. All passed without incident, much less revolution.[27]

The next testing of Government policy came in May, 1867, when Beales announced another giant Reform demonstration for Hyde Park. It was now clear that Walpole was hardly up to the demands of another confrontation. At Derby's insistence he reluctantly summoned a strategy meeting of the Cabinet, the Superintendent of Police, and the Law Officers for April 27. Hardy wrote in his diary: I never saw Walpole in such a way—he would suggest nothing."[28] With much reluctance and many misgivings, the Government decided that its only consistent course was another prohibition, and such was made public on May 1.[29] The Government's announced policy raised a predictable storm of controversy in the press and in the House. The National Reform League found increasing support for its opposition to the Government. Bright, impassioned as always, declared fervently in the House that in view of the peaceful demonstrations elsewhere, "it was monstrous that there could not be a similar meeting in a London park...without honourable Members...worrying the Home Secretary to swear in special constables and to take measures as if London were about to be sacked."[30] Hardy wrote in his diary: "Bright has absolutely urged violence and the Reform League seems inclined to adopt his course."[31]

Walpole spent the week prior to the confrontation deploying police, troops, and magistrates at strategic points in the park and in reinforcement positions and enrolling some twelve thousand special constables.[32] But police orders for May 6 reveal the hollow nature of this show of strength. No part of this huge force was empowered to take demonstrators into custody without the express direction of the Commissioner of Assistant Commissioner: no one was to use "offensive or angry language" toward the demonstrators, or to "prevent the assemblage of persons going to or away from Hyde Park." The response was to be a mammoth bluff.[33]

Hardy's diary betrays the indecision surfacing in Cabinet meetings on the Friday and Saturday prior to the Monday showdown: "We have our backs to the wall now." "On Saturday we had a Cabinet and agreed not quite with my assent to the course to be pursued tonight. I feel it will not satisfy the public but look rather like abdicating our functions. Still it must be admitted that the Law does not afford a very secure resting place for more."[34] Conservative demands for assurances of Governmental resistance reached a crescendo in the House on Friday, May 3. Out-of-doors, similar fear prevailed, illustrated by the resolution the Carlton Club sent to Disraeli: "It is right that you should know, if you do not know already, how very strong and outspoken is the feeling of the members of this Club against any vacillation, or any symptom of giving way on the part of the Government in the matter of the Hyde Park Demonstration tomorrow."[35]

Monday, May 6, turned out to be "a day of great heat and closeness which might well tempt people out in the cool of the evening if it ever was cool."[36] Over twelve thousand special constables supplemented some ten thousand police and military in a desperate show of power hopefully intended to overawe the demonstrators. Prodded by the defiant Bradlaugh, Beales called the Government's bluff, and proceeded in blatant defiance of Walpole's ban. While police and military looked on impassively, from 100,000 to 150,000 people joined the giant demonstration. There was no interruption or disturbance. The reformers' triumph was complete. So was the Government's humiliation. Its condemnation by Conservative elements may be illustrated by a resolution from the vestry of St. Leonard's Shoreditch expressing "...strong condemnation of the unwise, reckless, and vacillating conduct of the Government in issuing proclamations which it knew it had not the legal power to enforce, creating an alarm in the public mind by making unnecessary demonstrations of force against a peaceful movement of the people...."[37] Many in Lords and Commons charged the Government with self-contempt.[38] If July 23, 1866, had shown the Government unequal to mass confrontations in Hyde Park, May 6, 1867, proved that the Government had no longer even the will to resist.

In view of the overwhelming nature of the policy defeat, Walpole found it impossible to save face; his failure had been so public and so categorical. Hardy's diary recreates the scene in the Home Office the morning after:

> When I got to the office on Tuesday, Walpole immediately came in, in a state of deep depression, to tell me that he had felt he had, however unjustly, lost the confidence of his own friends and of the public and had resigned...he said he was so overdone that he really was not fit for his work, and would persist in going out.... He looked thoroughly broken down.[39]

That same morning Walpole sent his resignation to Derby, who immediately wrote to Disraeli: "His tone is so despondent...but his retirement *at this moment* would be inconvenient."[40] Derby naturally wished to avoid an additional admission of the Government's embarrassment, but Walpole had had enough. Reluctantly he remained in the Cabinet without office, a position he found almost as humiliating, and quite anomalous.[41] At Tuesday's Cabinet, "Nothing was said about Walpole, but he looked miserable. He is a just, good man but unfit for troublous times into which he has been cast...."[42] The Queen wrote "most kindly" to him concerning his resignation, and, never dreaming how onerous most Ministers regarded the privilege, sought to soften the blow by inviting him to Osborne as minister in attendance two weekends later!

From Balmoral, no doubt bolstered by the illiberal attitudes of the Queen, Walpole pleaded with his successor to remain firm, suggesting legislation making park meetings a misdemeanor, and warning against any proceeding "in which there might be the risk of failure." "Pray don't allow the preaching to go on."[43] But although Hardy attempted a renewed suppression, Bruce in 1872 settled the question for good by his Parks Act (see Chapter VII.)

The extent to which the demonstrations of the 1860s influenced the passage of the Reform Bill has become, of course, a subject of current debate.[44] But there can be no question that the Conservative prohibitions of the demonstrations of July 23,

1866, and May 6, 1867, resulted in clear-cut victories in the long war for the right of public meetings, and won the battle as far as Hyde Park was concerned.

1. PP XXIII (1856), "Report of the Royal Commission to inquire into the alleged disturbances of the public peace in Hyde Park, Sunday, July 1st, 1855; and the conduct of the metropolitan police in connection with the same." The Commissioners censured not only individual policemen but the orders of the Superintendent as well.

2. David Tribe, *President Charles Bradlaugh, M.P.* pp. 44–46. Quotation from *Autobiography of C. Bradlaugh* (1873), p. 12.

3. HO 45/A 43210, *Public Meetings in the Metropolis*, p. 14.

4. While the story of the franchise campaign is well known, it has usually been told from the political point of view, rather than from the vantage point of the Home Office, and the issue of public meeting.

5. *Annual Register* (1866), Part II, p. 97; Asa Briggs, *Victorian People* p. 204; Spencer Walpole, *The History of Twenty-Five Years*, II, p. 177.

6. Hypatia Bradlaugh Bonner [Charles' daughter] and J.M. Robertson, *Charles Bradlaugh*, Vol. I, pp. 222–225.

7. Cranbrook Papers: Dairy of John Stewart Gathorne-Hardy [son of the first Earl], HA 43: T 501/278; July 23, 1866. The Cranbrook Papers are housed in the Ipswich and East Suffolk County Record Office.

8. HO 41/20/207.

9. Bonner and Robertson, p. 224.

10. Henry Broadhurst, *Henry Broadhurst, M.P. The Story of His Life from a Stonemason's Bench to the Treasury Bench Told by Himself*, pp. 38, 39.

11. HO 45/O.S. 7854. Regiments used the evening of July 23 included the First and Second Life Guards, the Second Battalion Grenadier Guards, the Second Battalion Coldstream Guards, the First Battalion Scots Fusilier Guards. See also *Annual Register* (1866), II, p. 98.

12. Cranbrook Papers. Diary of John Hardy, July 24, 1886; Bonner and Robertson, p. 225.

13. HO 45/O.S. 7854. Regiments used the evening of July 24 included the Second Life Guards and two companies of the Coldstream Guards.

14. Cranbrook Papers. Diary of Gathorne-Hardy. HA 43: T 501/294.

15. This urgent request was not to be answered until Saturday the 28th, by which time the immediate problem was already solved.

16. The best account of this phase of the story is found in Royden Harrison, *Before the Socialists*, pp. 82 ff.

17. Cranbrook Papers. Diary of Gathorne-Hardy, July 26, 1866, HA 43: T 501/294.

18. Hughendon Papers. B/xx/5/357. Derby to Disraeli: July 26, 1866.

19. L.O.O. 231; July 28, 1866, written by H.M. Cairns and William Bovill.

20. Cranbrook Papers. Diary of Gathorne-Hardy, July 28 and 29, 1866, HA 43: T 501/298.

21. Gladstone Papers. B.M. Add. MSS. 44536, f 144.

22. Letter of Beales in *The Times*, July 28, 1866.

23. *Annual Register* (1866), II, pp. 138, 162, 179.

24. Bonner and Robertson, pp. 230, 231.

25. Ellenborough Papers. P.R.O. 30/21/4, Ellenborough to Derby, November 26, 1866.

26. HO 45/O.S./7854.

27. *Annual Register* (1886), II, p. 190.

28. Cranbrook Papers, Diary of Gathorne-Hardy, April 28, 1867; *Hughenden Papers*, B/XXI/W/73 Walpole to Disraeli, April 25, 1867.

29. HO 41/20/328; MEPOL 2/59.

30. *3 Hansard* CLXXXVII (May 3, 1867).

31. Cranbrook Papers. Diary of Gathorne-Hardy, April 26, 1867.

32. HO 41/20/322-327; HO 45/O.S. 7854/22.

33. HO 45/A4321o, p. 16.

34. Cranbrook Papers, Diary of Gathorne-Hardy, May 3 and 4, 1867.

35. Hughenden Papers. B/XI/J/129 Bateman to Disraeli, May 5, 1867; *3 Hansard* CLXXXVI (May 3, 1867).

36. Cranbrook Papers, Diary of Gathorne-Hardy, May 7, 1867.

37. HO 45/O.S. 7854/23 to which Walpole noted in pencil "A very intemperate Resolution." See also "The Conservative Surrender," *Quarterly Review* (October, 1867).

38. *3 Hansard* CLXXXVII (May 9, 1867).

39. Cranbrook Papers. Diary of Gathorne-Hardy, May 9, 1867.

40. Hughenden Papers. B/XX/5/429, Derby to Disraeli, May 7, 1867.

41. He would resign February 26, 1868.

42. Cranbrook Papers. Diary of Gathorne-Hardy, May 9, 1867.

43. Cranbrook Papers. T 501/260; Walpole to Hardy, May 30, 1867.

44. See especially Royden Harrison, *Before the Socialists*, who emphasizes their revolutionary threat, and Maurice Cowling, *1867: Disraeli, Gladstone and Revolution*, F.B. Smith, *The Making of the Second Reform Bill*, and Gertrude Himmelfarb, "The Politics of Democracy: The English Reform Act of 1867," *Journal of British Studies* (November, 1966), who place less stress upon the revolutionary possibilities.

5

THOSE RIOTOUS ELECTIONS

The student of British elections notices "tumults" as early as 1450,[1] and, in the absence of strong deterrents, electorial rioting (legally a form of "intimidation") increased through the centuries along with bribery and corruption. By the nineteenth century the turbulence of election campaigns was an acknowledged though routinely deplored aspect of British life, best illustrated in Hogarth's famous series of election prints.[2] Norman Gash has delineated the rowdy and violent character of politics in *Politics in the Age of Peel*, traits which persisted long afterward.[3] So it was with singular nonchalance that John Bright described an 1865 by-election at Rochdale as "...a hotly fought affair. The town was very excited all the week; much fighting and drinking—as usual under our system of elections."[4] It was not till the second Reform Era that Britain came seriously to grips with the problems of electoral malpractice.[5] This chapter examines the role played by crowds in the five general elections surrounding the enactment of Britain's most stringent malpractice controls.

The general election of 1865 was intensely contested on the local level, the 204 contests doubling the number of the previous general election year of 1859. Mob rioting was widespread, the most scandalous of the disturbances occurring at Nottingham where a mob of thirty thousand swarmed through the market place, smashing windows and hurling rotten vegetables. The reading of the Riot Act failed to prevent the sacking of the Liberal party headquarters, and it was only with the aid of two detachments of cavalry troops that the authorities restored order. One of the victorious Conservative candidates, Sir Robert Clifton, lost his seat the following year to a Parliamentary committee because he had urged his supporters to prevent the Liberals' packing of the polling booths and had threatened "We will butcher them; and when we have butchered and Cayenne peppered them the public will not give a penny a pound for them."[6] Other disturbances occurred at Rotherham and Chippenham where rival mobs destroyed a total of fifty houses during the campaign.[7] A Royal Commission heard evidence for two years on thirty-five election petitions and conccluded that corrupt practices still existed.[8] Just three months before the next general election Commons passed the Elections Petitions and Corrupt Practices at Elections Act which transferred the trials from the Commons to a panel of judges from the three chief common law courts: Queen's Bench, Exchequer, and Common Pleas.[9]

The general election of 1868 featured an enlarged electorate, an unusually lengthy campaign, the issue of the disestablishment of the Irish Church, and again a significant amount of mob violence.[10] Some of the most serious disorders broke out in Lancashire where Murphyism had already kindled an explosive atmosphere during the spring and summer.[11] In Blackburn the day before the municipal election rival mobs, thoroughly liquored by treating, fought freely in the streets and destroyed the committee rooms of each candidate. The *Annual Register* described the scene the following day at the Trinity Ward polling place:

> A cart of stones was kept in readiness by the blue and orange [Tory] party, and a crowd of women kept supplying them with missiles. Most of the rioters were armed with picking sticks about two feet in length and 1 1/2 inches thick at the head. They appeared to have been newly made.... All along the pavement streams of blood were flowing, and the sickening sight of men with blood flowing from their heads and faces met one at every turn. The police charged the mob with drawn cutlasses and truncheons, committing great havoc; but they did not succeed in restoring even comparative quiet for a long time.... Business was interrupted at the polls for hours.... [12]

Blackburn's schools were turned into hospitals to accommodate the injured. Hartington headed a Select Committee to investigate. The mayor of Stalybridge testified that his borough "lay under a perfect reign of terror" from August to November. At Ashton-under-Lyne fierce street fighting raged uncontrolled despite the combined efforts of local police, special constables, and the military. At Bradford one man had his eye cut out when struck by a piece of iron. The crowd at Bradford numbered seventy thousand at Nomination Day.[13] Bristol witnesses told of Liberal agents from London who organized and paid "flying columns" of two to three hundred men armed with bludgeons who drove off Conservative voters from polling places, the customary flaunting of party colors facilitating party identification.[14] Old-timers compared the violence to that of 1831. A magistrate at Cardiff was felled by stones while reading the Riot Act. Many serious disturbances broke out in the iron-working towns of Monmouthshire; crowds gutted a hotel at Blaenavon. The Select Committee concluded that intimidation by mobs had prevailed "to a considerable extent," and that nomination days in particular were too frequently attended with "riot,... drunkenness, and violence,"[15] *The Times* cynically described a typical nomination day:

> We all know what a nomination day is like. The presiding functionary bespeaks a fair hearing for both sides, and it is well if he gets to the end of his few sentences without derisive cheers and ironical cries explicable only by a local historian. After that no one gets a hearing. Unceasing clamour prevails; proposers, seconders, and candidates speak in dumb show, or confide their sentiments to the reporters; heads are broken, blood flows from numerous noses, and the judgment of the electors is generally subjected to a severe training as a preliminary to the voting of the following day.[16]

Most of the committee's recommendations were incorporated into the Ballot Act (Parliamentary and Municipal Elections Act) which abolished public nominations, increased the number of polling places, and introduced the secret ballot. A companion Corrupt Practices Act stipulated that public houses might not be used as committee rooms during election campaigns.[17]

The first general election to test the effectiveness of the new legislation took place in February, 1874, following a surprise dissolution and a campaign of only three weeks. But the continued prevalence of crowd violence was evidenced in the endless pages of testimony contained in the petition trials and four investigative Select Committees, best summarized by Cornelius O'Leary.[18] Gangs of bricklayers and miners from Manchester invaded some of the small towns of North Durham engaging in street fighting with both rival mobs and police. Irish gangs wrecked the polling at Dudley. A Wolverhampton mob routed the local police force and threatened to kill the magistrate who was trying to read the

Riot Act. Thirty Wolverhampton Tories invaded Willenhead and clashed with Liberal gangs there:

> Blood flowed freely and they were terribly kicked, one so shockingly about the head and face that his life is in much jeopardy.... So soon as the roughs were able they got back to the railway station, where the profuse flow of blood has left painful evidence of the extent of the injuries... [19]

J.L. Gavin characterized the election at Sheffield as "among the most savage and disorderly of Victorian times," perhaps because a red herring struck Joseph Chamberlain full in the face while he was speaking in the central square.[20]

The best account of the many scattered but serious riots attending the election of 1880 may be found in the work of a Liberal journalist, William Saunders, himself later a Member for Walworth.[21] Saunders' graphic work describes over twenty disturbances involving the usual street fighting, window smashing, personal injuries, police confrontations, and a burning in effigy (of Disraeli). Each party charged the other with incitement, as *The Times* remarked: "If the secret electioneering history of the country ever came to be written, we doubt whether either party would be able to cry 'shame' on the other."[22]

Despite the Corrupt Practices Act of 1883, the most stringent ever to be enacted in Britain, the violence accompanying the campaign of 1885 was, if anything, greater than that which preceded it. Aggressive mobs attacked the police in Somerset, Sussex, Glamorgan, Suffolk, Nottingham. Curfews were declared in Cornwall. Lime-throwing blinded some residents of Dartford. Several hundred colliers demolished eighteen houses and two hotels in the Tory section of Radstock and repeatedly attacked local police and later Bristol reinforcements. Candidates were beaten up in Denbigh, Buckingham, Hereford. The Suffolk County Police were reportedly at bay for days at a time. A Glamorganshire laborer urged a polling-day crowd of one thousand to kill the constables trying to restore order. *The Times* remarked succinctly: "Never was there such a hurly burly."[23]

In view of all this disorder the degree of effectiveness which Cornelius O'Leary credits the Act of 1883 must be questioned: "Riots and disturbances had occurred with monotonous regularity before 1883, afterwards the individual heckler became a feature of electioneering. Public drunkenness was almost a thing of the past; and likewise organized intimidation."[24] O'Leary has been misled by the use of the petition trials as "the main barometer of electoral morality" when in actual practice only a minute fraction of election riots ever appeared in petitions. In the 1885 campaign just referred to, only one petition charged riotous intimidation. Horsham appears only once in the petition trials from 1832 to 1885 although Albery has shown all forms of corruption present in varying degrees in every election of these years.[25] For one thing rioting was the most difficult litigation to prove against an opponent, and furthermore any violence suffered by the victorious party would naturally go unchallenged. Hanham and Gwyn have demonstrated the "financial nightmare" a petition posed for all parties.[26] Actually the greatest effect of the Act was to reduce drastically the number of petitions lodged: only thirty for the four general elections following the Act compared to 162 for the four preceding.[27] It is evident that petitions, while providing concrete evidence for the presence of disorder, cannot serve to document its absence.

A most casual survey tallied seventy-one separate incidents of serious disorder which broke out in conjunction with election campaigns from 1865 to 1885, each causing substantial property damage and/or personal injury. There were, however, no recorded fatilities. It was in the small towns and rural areas that the great majority of election disturbances occurred and it was there that the absence as yet of any effective policing was most conspicuous. Where the police constituted a defensible force, they attempted to control the rioting as best they could, but in most instances the crowd attacked them with far greater fury and with more formidable weapons than they the people. At Leamington a crowd advanced upon the local police armed with knives and pokers. Frequently the crowd turned upon the police after routing their rival crowd, but just as frequently challenging the police appeared to be a primary goal. A Liberal crowd at Exmouth, intent on expunging from the town every trace of the Conservatives' color (in this case, blue), fell upon the local police and doused them and their blue uniforms with flour.[28] The most sanguinary threats were as commonly directed against police as against campaign rivals.

The customary campaign practice of treating individuals to drinks simply exacerbated the perennial Victorian problem of drunkenness. As the size of the electorate increased, bribery of individuals became economically unfeasible and was replaced by increased wholesale treating on a community-wide basis. Until the Act of 1872 most local parties quartered their committee rooms in or near public houses to facilitate this practice. Both parties were routinely guilty of indiscriminate treating, although the partisan "torrent of beer and gin" which allegedly swept away the Liberals in the election of 1874 is still an eminently disputable question.[29] Treating and drunkenness constituted by far the most frequent charges in election petitions of these years. It was common for candidates to make commitments to public houses to pay for whatever drinks were dispensed during the polling period. Albery's picture of Horsham at election time shows every public house thronged with disorderly people eager to drink at another's expense.[30]

The unabated mob disturbances which persisted in the wake of the preventive statutes of 1854, 1872 and 1883 suggests quite clearly that the phenomenon was far less related to the malfunctioning of electoral machinery than were the other forms of corruption. Some of the most serious riots exploded after the declaration of the poll, as at Horsham in 1868, Dover at a by-election in 1871, Leamington and Shaftesbury in 1880, Buckley in 1885. In a typical victory celebration in Bristol in 1868 the victorious solicitor astride a white horse led an exultant Liberal parade through the streets, the crowd smashing windows of opponents' properties.[31] It cannot be assumed that all electoral violence grew out of a genuine though overly enthusiastic concern for influencing the outcome of the poll. Many of the most serious disorders seem entirely extraneous to the campaign and the polling, spontaneous outbursts of sheer ebullience.

Asa Briggs saw Victorian electioneering providing a unique opportunity for drinking free beer and indulging in "petty violence of every kind."[32] The magnetic attraction of excitement for its own sake cannot be minimized, especially in an era notoriously deficient in public amusements.[33] It has been frequently noted that politics constituted the national Victorian pastime and J.R. Vincent has gone so far as to say that what the country desired was "the election victory itself, as a visceral thrill."[34] In the fevered atmosphere surrounding an election campaign the most trivial incident sufficed to set off a full-scale disturbance. A typical instance occurred in Ripley in 1868 when rival crowds collided in a fierce encounter after a Tory tied a blue ribbon to his dog's tail and set him loose in the marketplace.[35] For the people of a small town such as Horsham, Albery was convinced that elections provided "almost the only occasions... for letting off a little steam, and that they used these occasions as a license to throw away such self-respect as at other times would cry shame to them for such behavior."[36]

The prevailing Victorian attitude toward electoral rambunctiousness was singularly cavalier. Few were genuinely scandalized or even surprised by reports of electoral disorders. Toward the close of the 1885 polling *The Times* wrote:

> The hubbub which is now abating might have suggested that the Kingdom had gone irrecoverably out of its wits with political frenzy. ...The country was able without danger to act as if it were momentarily insane because it felt itself essentially sane at bottom. A nation without settled political instincts and habits could not have let itself run wild, as has been the recent pleasure of Englishmen.... At the termination of the engagement he returns to his ordinary avocations. He acts as if there were peace in the land; and so it will be found after this week.... A good fight at intervals of four or five or six years is very well.[37]

In 1900 William Redmond stated in the House of Commons:

> I should be the last person in the world to complain... of the storming of an election meeting and the taking of the platform. I think that is one of the most interesting features of electioneering. If for the future every election meeting was to be conducted with the decorum of a Quaker's gathering,... political life would have lost most of its charm...[38]

1. In connection with a county election in Huntington: Cornelius O'Leary, *The Elimination of Corrupt Practices in British Elections 1868-1911*, p.7.

2. See Joseph Grego, *History of Parliamentary Elections and Electioneering In the Old Days*.

3. Norman Gash, *Politics In the Age of Peel*, pp. 137-153. Asa Briggs describes Victorian election as "...sordid and corrupt exercises in bribery, cajolery and violence." *Victorian People*, p. 108.

4. John Bright, *The Diaries of John Bright*, p. 289.

5. In 1835 Commons had established a Select Committee to study the most effective means of combatting bribery, corruption and intimidation:

PP (1835) VIII, and in 1854 the Corrupt Practices Prevention Act (17 & 18 Vict., c 102) penalized intimidation with fines of £50.

6. *PP* Vol. VIII (1868–1869), p. 41; *Morning Herald* (London) July 13, 1865; *The Times*, April 4, 1866.

7. *PP* Vol. VIII (1868–1869), p. 182; *Morning Herald* (London) July 25, 1865; Bright, p. 289.

8. *PP* Vols. XXVII–XXX (1867).

9. 31 & 32 Vict., c 125.

10. Testimony regarding the mob violence in the election country-wide may be found in Great Britain, *Parliamentary Papers*, Vol. VIII (1868–1869), "Report From the Select Committee on Parliamentary and Municipal Elections." For an analysis of the election in Lancashire, H.J. Hanham, *Elections And Party Management: Politics In the Time of Disraeli and Gladstone*, pp. 284–322.

11. See Chapter III.

12. *Annual Register* (1868), Part II, pp. 135–136.

13. *PP* Vol. VIII (1868–1869). See also *Leeds Mercury*, November 24, 1868; *Spectator*, November 28, 1868; *West Sussex Gazette*, November 19, 1868.

14. *PP* Vol. VIII (1868–1869), p. 167. For the role of the election agent see E.A. Smith, "The Election Agent In English Politics 1734–1832" *EHR*, LXXIV (1969), pp. 12–35 and for the later period, Hanham, pp. 233–248.

15. *PP* Vol. VIII (1868–1869), XIII–XVII, 181–196. See also *3 Hansard*, CCII (1868), 1355 ff.

16. *The Times*, June 23, 1868.

17. 35 & 36 Vict., c 33.

18. O'Leary, pp. 88–111.

19. *The Times*, February 5–19, 1874. For brief descriptions of the disturbances in Staffordshire, see *Annual Register* (1874), Chr., 12.

20. J.L. Garvin, *Life of Joseph Chamberlain*, I, pp. 166, 167.

21. William Saunders, *The New Parliament: 1880*, pp. 230–235. See also *PP* Vol. LVIII (1880); Vol. XL (1881).

22. *The Times*, March 31, 1880.

23. *PP* (1886), Vol. LII, 323–337; *The Times*, November 27–December 10, 1885.

24. O'Leary, p. 208.

25. William Albery, *A Parliamentary History of the Ancient Borough of Horsham 1295–1885*, p. 490.

26. Hanham, pp. 258–260; William Gwyn, *Democracy and the Cost of Politics in Britain*, pp. 86, 87.

27. *3 Hansard*, CCII (1868), 1355 ff.

28. Saunders, p. 231 (in 1880).

29. The evidence of W.H. Maehl ("The British General Election of 1874," unpublished dissertation, University of Chicago, 1957) points to systematic anti-Government campaigning on the part of the public houses and the Licensed Victuallers associations, but Hanham has disputed the effectiveness of such influence on economic grounds (pp. 222–225). See also R.C.K. Ensor, *England 1870–1914*, pp. 21–22; M. Ostrogorsky, *Democracy and the Organization of Political Parties* (1908), I, pp. 478 ff.

30. *PP* Vol. VIII (1875) "Report of Select Committee on Corrupt Practices Prevention and Election Petitions Acts," Minutes of Evidence, pp. 137 ff.; Albery, p. 439.

31. O'Leary, p. 46; *PP* Vol. VIII (1868-1869), p. 196.

32. Asa Briggs, *Victorian People*, p. 111.

33. See Trevor Lloyd, *The General Election of 1880*, p. 90; Ostrogorsky, I, p. 466.

34. J.R. Vincent, *Pollbooks: How Victorians Voted*, p. 47.

35. *Leeds Mercury*, November 21, 1868.

36. Albery, p. 434.

37. *The Times*, December 9, 1885.

38. *4 Hansard*, LXXX (1900), 973.

6

DIRTY DICK'S ARMY

What William Murphy was to Catholicism, William Booth became to the late Victorian public house. Combining the moral fervor of a John Wesley with a native gift for showmanship, Booth parlayed a little-known "Christian Mission" onto an evangelical crusade that reached around the world. As a young Wesleyan preacher he had developed a rare natural talent for dynamic preaching, but his flair for the flamboyant and the unorthodox soon alienated him from the main body of Wesleyans. By the age of thirty-two he had become an independent street preacher in London's East End. Booth soon became convinced that the arch-enemy was devil inspired liquor, and the single most critical factor responsible for the physical penury and moral degradation of the population. Liquor establishments abounded in East London, in many streets outnumbering all other businesses. There were perhaps over 100,000 pubs in all of London in the 1880s. Some offered penny glasses of gin, especially for children. From the streets and corners of the East End, Booth courageously proclaimed his peculiar message of salvation through abstinence.

In 1878 the always-ingenious Booth conceived a bold promotional scheme, the transformation of his tiny following into a military order. He became "General Booth"; his followers took military ranks, complete with uniforms and flags and standards; orders were couched in military terms. The Salvation Army was born. Almost instant success attended this novel experiment and by 1883 there were over three hundred corps in the United Kingdom and the Army had made landings on the continent, in America, and even Australia. *The War Cry* boasted a circulation of over 300,000.

Catherine Booth had early overcome a natural reticence about public appearances to take her place beside her husband in pulpits and on the streets. Large numbers of women eagerly joined the Army, dubbed the "Hallelujah Lasses" or the "Happy Eliza's," the latter name deriving from a promotional stunt in which a lieutenant Eliza Haynes paraded through Nottingham brandishing a placard announcing "I am Happy Eliza." The Booths' son, Bramwell, also joined the family campaign at a surprisingly young age.

The Booths became expert showmen, and each publicity stunt proved more outlandish than the last. A Lieutenant at Scarborough (Yorkshire) arrived in town riding on a donkey robed in crimson and ringing a bell. An ex-convict preached the Salvationist message in a convict uniform. Bramwell rose from a coffin asking, "Death, where is thy sting?" Other preachers lectured in goatskins, bare-footed nineteenth-century John the Baptists. But the Booths' most successful technique proved to be the military-style parades, which also earned them the greatest opposition from otherwise neutral residents. The Sunday processions drew up to fifty thousand marchers and the inevitable collisions between Booth's Army and the local opponents were tantamount to full-scale neighborhood warfare. The handling of this delicate problem by local magistrates and the Home Office demonstrated again the limits to which popular opinion on the one hand and government policy on the other might stretch the right to public assembly and procession.

The Salvationist street gatherings and parades were engineered to evoke rousing enthusiasm rather than sober reflection. Well-known Christian hymns were sung to drinking tunes such as, "Here's to good old whisky" and "Champagne Charlie is my name." "Why should the devil have all the best tunes?" explained Booth. The raucous music and the colorful banners and streamers helped to create a carnival, even a Corybantic atmosphere much resented by those of staider tastes. An exasperated Londoner complained to *The Times* in 1882:

> Our usual quiet Sunday evening was unbearable. Shoutings and ravings were followed with cries of 'Hallelujah! Amen! Amen!' and then said the preacher, 'Give 'em that chorus again.' A band struck up in which the drum, cornet, and harmonium were distinguishable, ac-

companied by the loud chorus and occasional stamping of the hundreds assembled. 'Abide with me' was followed by 'Auld Lang Syne,' while the surging roar of the mob in Oxford Street was dreadful.[1]

It was much the same in rural areas. An elderly resident of Worthing (Sussex) echoed the increasingly vocal complaint in 1884: "Every Sunday they [the Salvationists] perambulated the street singing and shouting at the top of their voices, and beating tambourines to the great annoyance of the peaceable inhabitants."[2] The unorthodox methods employed by The Salvation Army for the conversion of "sinners" scandalized high churchmen, though the Archbishop of Canterbury conceded in the House of Lords that, "... their peculiar mode of proceeding was such as might have considerable influence over uncultivated minds."[3]

An uncompromising opposition also sprang naturally enough from the ranks of the brewers and the publicans who, it was said, promoted local anti-Salvationist gangs dubbed the "Skeleton Army." Its roughs at first merely heckled the Salvationists, but in time the skull and crossbones of the Skeleton Army's black flag came to represent a more physical interference. Salvationist meetings were disrupted; their parades were broken up. In the early 1880s physical attacks increased alarmingly. The Skeleton Army pelted the Salvation marchers with mud, stones, dead cats, paint, even live coals. The Army attributed its persecution to "a spirit of ruffianism now so rife."[4]

One of the more awkward aspects of the problem was that the local police, many of whom were individually opposed to the Army, were forced to surrender holidays and Sundays to protect the marchers. It was therefore not to be expected that the protection thus rendered would be very enthusiastic. Frequently the police assigned to protect the Salvation Army were themselves subscribers to the funding of the Skeleton Army. Much to their increasing frustration, the Salvationist victims found themselves under arrest rather than their attackers. It was decided to appeal directly to the Home Office.

The Home Secretary in Gladstone's second ministry was William Vernon Harcourt, born at York in 1827, the grandson of an Archbishop. The family traced its ancestry to the Plantagents. After the customary years at Cambridge and Lincoln's Inn, Harcourt entered Commons as Member for Oxford in 1868, joining the

Sir William Harcourt

government as solicitor-general in 1873. A prolific writer, a masterful public speaker, Jeffersonian in his interests, Harcourt was one of the most polished and erudite politicians of his time. His first in Classics shows in the Greek and Latin quotes sprinkled so freely throughout his memos and correspondence, many in the Greek script and untranslated or even transliterated. His letters abound in allusions—biblical, classical, literary—but in a hand almost indecipherable. The strong liberalizing influence of education and experience overcame a deep instinctual preference for oligarchy. "He would give anything to have lived in the last century", Hamilton noted in his diary,[5] but the thrust of his efforts lifelong was decidedly liberal. He urged franchise reform in 1866, commutation of Fenian death sentences, attacked his own party's Parks Bill in 1872 as an infringement of the right of public meeting, opposed capital punishment, advocated more lenient sentences for every offender except Irish terrorists and the London dynamiters, and in general permitted rather than prohibited. The Queen was perennially critical of his exercise of the prerogative of reprieve and remission and judges and local J.P.s were outraged by his proverbial leniency toward more venial offenders. "He put humanity above the law," was the way his personal secretary put it, and Bright proclaimed him "the most humane Home Secretary he had encountered."[6]

The first instance of Salvation Army harrassment came before the Home Office in 1881. Fourteen Salvationists of Salisbury (including three Councillors) appealed to Harcourt claiming three years' persecution at the hands of the local mob and futile requests for police protection. The Home Office routinely asked for a report on the matter from the mayor, whose personal animosity to the Army quickly became clear. Although he claimed twenty-two convictions against anti-Salvationists during the prior three years, it was apparent he viewed the marchers as a silly annoyance and that only the most grudging police protection had been offered. Salisbury's police force numbered only fourteen. Besides, the mayor's argument ran, what is to prevent any other group desirous of parading from demanding similar protection? It would seem unfair to ask the ratepayers to support an augmented police force merely to accommodate a minority. The mayor's position was that order could be maintained easily if the Salvation Army would stop parading. "The remedy is so obviously in the hands of the Salvationists themselves as has been repeatedly pointed out to them."[7] Much to the astonishment of the petitioners, the liberal Harcourt seemed to share this unsympathetic attitude. He formally denied their appeals on grounds that local police could not secure such processions from molestation. Meanwhile the anti-Salvationists of Salisbury formed a "Society to stop the parading of the streets by the Salvation Army," and threatened a blanket blockade of the processions.

On the 23rd of February matters had reached such an impasse that the mayor and town clerk of Salisbury met in person with the Home Secretary to ascertain precise governmental policy on the question. After consulting with Liddell, Harcourt advised that the processions be banned if the magistrates anticipate a riot due to the foolish conduct of a body of persons in persisting in parading, the ban to be enforced by local and county police and special constables if necessary. This decision was based on Bruce's memo to Liverpool authorities during the threatened Fenian and Orange processions there in 1869. On receipt of Harcourt's letter the Salisbury authorities banned all Salvation Army processions in the town.

Similar developments took place throughout the country during 1881; those at Basingstoke (Hants) were particularly well documented.[8] As at other places, the Basingstoke Salvation Army had so antagonized the local populace by frequent parades as to elicit not only verbal heckling but outright physical disruption. The Army's prosecution of a number of their attackers in March evoked a "Declaration of War against Dirty Dick's Army," and plans for a decisive confrontation in the market place the following Sunday (March 20). A huge crowd of townspeople thus assembled at ten o'clock next Sunday morning and marched under the Union Jack to intercept the Salvation Army cavalcade. Although the Army marchers changed course twice to avoid their opponents, the townspeople succeeded in engaging them in a pitched battle. The Union Jack went down as the Salvationists successfully battled their way to the market place but were unable to maintain their position there for long. Amid scenes of general confusion the Army retreated to headquarters on the outskirts of town.

In the afternoon the townsmen, their flag and pole now re-paired, reassembled in the market place. Gamely, the Salvationists ventured forth from the security of their factory-headquarters and started again towards the center of town. The townsmen intercepted them this time in Church Square, where the worst rioting of the day occurred. The desperate collision of these determined forces on the Square led to a general mélee involving thousands, including Mayor Blatch, the largest brewer in town. Despite much superficial bloodshed, there were no injuries more serious than broken limbs. The mayor had sworn in one hundred constables but three-fourths protested against having to protect the Salvationists and many simply refused to do so "because they had their best Sunday clothes on." There was good reason to fear that the specials who did serve might join the mob in attacking those they were commissioned to protect. At this point Mayor Blatch appealed to the Home Office for advice, and upon receipt of suggestions similar to those Harcourt had sent to Salisbury, the magistrates immediately banned all Salvation Army processions in Basingstoke.

The Army resolved to test the legality of the ban but could not obtain assurances of police protection even for this purpose. On April 2 (1881) William Booth protested to Harcourt that "...the magistrates have given us to understand that we shall get no protection from the mob on Sunday, and the special constables armed with truncheons will be left to join the rabble in attacking our people and doing what they say they will do, 'break their heads.' Now what is to be done if there is no right of public right of assembly [sic] in the open spaces and streets of this country; the sooner we know it the better; but surely some protection can be afforded to us while we proceed to obtain the opinion of the properly constituted legal authorities."[9]

Not only did police turn back the next Sunday procession, but deprived the Army even of its test case through the simple expe-dient of not arresting anyone, to the huge dismay of Army leaders. Mayor Blatch continued to enforce the prohibition until August when a newly-appointed town Council outvoted him five to two. The five magistrates viewed such a ban as "an interference with liberty" and placed the blame for the riots squarely on a band of young roughs, paid agents of the liquor interests of Basingstoke.

The Salvation Army processions thus resumed but met with the same disruption as before. Harcourt reiterated his position that it was the duty of local authorities to "prevent any proceedings which are calculated to produce disorder," but the issue remained clouded. In response to appeals from local authorities facing similar difficultues all over southern England, Harcourt sent the identical formula:

> While it is the duty of the local magistrates by every means in their power to preserve the public peace, they must at the same time exercise their discretion, depending on all the local circumstances, as to whether the conduct of a body of persons in persisting in parading the streets is likely to produce a riot or serious disturbance of the peace. Such processions, not being illegal in themselves, cannot, in the absence of other circumstances, be legally prevented; but where they provoke antagonism and lead to riotous collisions, and where the peace of the town would be endangered if they are allowed to continue, the magistrates should by every means in their power endeavour to prevent them. If, therefore, the justices have reason to believe that these processions, if permitted, will lead to a breach of the peace, they should at once cause a sworn information to be laid before them by the chief constable, showing grounds why, in his judgment, if the processions continue, a breach of the peace, and probably a riot, will be the result. They should then issue notices and promulgate them, to the effect that such information having been laid before them on oath, they give notice to all persons who intend to take part in such processions that the procession cannot be permitted to take place. They should call upon all the leaders of the movement to prevent them, and upon all peaceably-disposed persons to abstain from joining them, and upon all persons to abstain from collecting a crowd for the purpose of interfering with the procession. They should, when about to prevent the processions, endeavour to collect sufficient force to enable them to prevent any assembly from forming by getting assistance from the county police and swearing in special constables. The forming of the procession should be stopped, each person being told the reason why it will not be allowed; and they should be urged to disperse quietly before force is used. The people should be made to understand, as far as possible, that the processions are not permitted for fear of collision and breach of the peace. If, however, in spite of every effort, the attempt to form a procession is persevered in, force may be used to prevent it, and care should be taken that sufficient force for that purpose is at hand. It is easier to prevent a procession from forming than to deal with an excited mob after a collision has taken place.[10]

Harcourt's formula solved little as the disturbances persisted across the country. A woman Salvationist nearly died and a man suffered total blindness in 1882, both victims of anti-Army rioting at Chester.[11] But less serious injuries were more common. At Crediton (Devon) members of the Skeleton Army accosted a band of

Salvationists in a carriage, cut the reins, loosened a wheel, and sent the carriage and occupants hurtling down a hillside. At Salisbury townspeople surrounded an Army procession and doused the marchers with bags of flour and rotten eggs.[12] In some towns Salvationists were arrested for marching and at other places their attackers were arrested. Fines and prison terms were meted out according to the sentiments of local authorities. In 1882, eighty-six Salvationists, including fifteen women, were sent to prison while 660 others suffered injuries at the hands of local mobs.

Ultimately one of the convicted Salvationists, Beatty, appealed and the Court of the Queen's Bench, on June 13, 1882, sustained his case. The judgment by Justice J. Field: "What has happened here is that an unlawful organization has assumed to itself the right to prevent the appellants and others from lawfully assembling together, and the finding of the justices amounts to this, that a man may be convicted for doing a lawful act if he knows that his doing it may cause another to do an unlawful act. There is no authority for such a proposition."[13] In the wake of the Beatty decision and a revised Law Officers Opinion (#690), Harcourt was forced to reverse himself and direct local authorities that Salvation Army processions were entitled to full police protection. He did allow himself the advice that persuasion to desist might still be employed, and in Commons he persisted in his contention that magistrates of towns with less than stout forces ought to retain some legal power to prevent collisions between rival groups.[14]

It is not difficult to explain why this staunch civil libertarian adopted such an illiberal stance with regard to the Salvation Army. His high church preferences no doubt prejudiced him against them on religious ground. On the temperance question, he stood for local option. But Harcourt's predominant ideal was civic harmony and community order. To Harcourt's way of thinking the Army marchers were not only ill-advised and ludicrous, they were disruptive. Their leaders were uncompromising. Their foolish antics seem to have blinded Harcourt to the infringement of personal liberties which were at stake.

The Beatty decision confirmed the Army's contention that its processions were legal but did little to discourage its attackers. Local police were not everywhere strong enough to guarantee protection, as at seashore towns such as Folkestone where summer-time crowds numbered in the thousands and the police force numbered sixteen. In 1883 local authorities applied for County Police but were denied: "Sorry cannot meet your wishes—so many calls upon the Force at this time." A request was then made to Scotland Yard for twelve mounted constables and twenty-four on foot and this too was denied.[15] Similar troubles beset the Army at Brighton where police were unable to prevent repeated assaults and disturbances.[16] Much of this behavior may be attributable to mere summer horseplay.

The unpopularity of the Salvationists in Derby flared into a series of ugly riots in August, 1885. When Salvation Army contingents from several neighboring towns met in Derby on the 17th, six to seven thousand townspeople soundly trounced them in a vicious hand-to-hand mélee in the market place, then shattered every window in the Salvation Army barracks and smashed the band instruments. The following evening the triumphant townspeople celebrated their victory by overturning several crates of rotten pears in the market place and hurling them in all directions.[17]

In 1888 the Skeleton Army of Chipping Norton (Oxford) ceremoniously marched to its encounter with the Salvationsists behind a draped coffin. In several serious collisons, both male and female Salvation Army processionists suffered injuries. The Army charged it had requested greater police protection, and that it was refused. The Chief Constable of Oxford explained that he had only four men available for duty at Norton.[18]

Processions in London were customarily accompanied by adequate police protection and few serious collisions occurred there. The London Skeleton Army was described as "chiefly youths of the lowest class." One attacker was a Frederick Marsh, labourer, aged thirty, fined in January of 1883 ten shillings or seven days in jail for stone-throwing. He was also found to have in his possession "a leather strap with several brass knuckles."[19]

Following the 1882 court decision, many authorities resorted to charges of highway or traffic obstruction against the Salvation Army. In 1887 at Stamford five Salvationists received twenty-one days imprisonment each for holding a meeting one Sunday evening in the market place. The technical charge was "obstructing the highway." At Warwick the same year the Salvationists held meetings in the Corn Market, and three were fined on the same charge. But use of traffic obstruction statutes was hardly uniform. In London in June, 1889, a mass procession of the Salvation Army, disregarding police directives, thronged the Strand between 5:00 and 6:00 P.M., not only causing a monumental traffic jam, but also breaking windows, waving cumbersome banners, and accidentally injuring the chief police inspector. In this case, the police did not arrest anyone, while magistrates of Whitchurch (Hants) that same summer convicted seventeen members of the Army for obstruction of traffic.[20] Nor were magistrates and police impartial in their enforcement of the laws on traffic obstruction, for there were countless street preachers all over London whose obstruction the police never seemed to notice. In 1887 Charles Bradlaugh invited the Home Secretary for a ride in a cab some Sunday to see two or three hundred undisturbed meetings of street preachers in places where the traffic was obviously impeded.[21]

Opponents of the Army parades searched local statute books for other laws which might trip up the Salvationists. In June of 1888 there occurred a collision in High Street between a horse-drawn carriage and a Salvation Army procession with flags and band, "many of the members wearing gaudy clothes." A citizens' petition was sent to the Local Board of Health demanding that it ban such processions in High Street under the Public Health Act, a course rejected in a subsequent legal opinion.[22] Torquay officials found that section 36 of the Torquay Harbour and District Act of 1886 gave the local Board of Works authority to prohibit noisy processions on Sunday, and upon this basis they sent over twenty Salvationist marchers to prison in March and April of 1888.[23] That same year Commons found this a gross abuse of the Act's intent and repealed section 36 of the Act.[24] Carlisle (Cumberland) and Reading (Berks) passed local laws permitting the mayor to prohibit Sunday processions whenever he saw fit, and Colchester's Town Council (Essex) passed a by-law forbidding open-air processions on both Saturdays and Sundays.[25]

In the early nineties the southern beach resort of Eastbourne (Sussex) became the scene of an embittered struggle among the Salvation Army, the local mob, and the Town Council. An obscure clause (169) of the Eastbourne Improvement Act of 1885 had pro-

hibited on Sunday any street processions that were accompanied
by instrumental music. Under this Act Eastbourne's mayor in
June, 1891, banned all such processions, and police arrested forty-
seven Salvationists during that month alone for violation of clause
169.[26] The Salvationists promptly discarded their instruments
and paraded as before. Meanwhile, Commons repealed clause 169
(June, 1892).[27] As the mobs continued their attacks upon the
Salvation Army, Eastbourne's police force of thirty-eight strained
to maintain order. In the middle of July the staunchly anti-Army
Town Council voted to withdraw all special police protection from
the Army's controversial processions, but the Home Department
refused to sanction this action. During the ensuing six months,
practically the whole of Eastbourne's police force struggled to
protect the Army, and on nine occasions county police had to
augment their ranks at a cost of over £ 157, of which the Army
paid nothing. In spite of this, on several subsequent collisions the
Eastbourne mob successfully disrupted the Salvation Army processions.[28]

After years of persecution and obstruction, the determined
groups who had sung "We Shall Conquer" so tirelessly and dog-
gedly did just that. By 1898 the Army was assisting daily over
18,000 needy persons, and earned the praise of the Lord Mayor
of the City of London. Edward VII received "General" Booth
in June of 1904 and Queen Alexandra donated £ 1,000 to the
Salvation Army the following year. In October, 1905, Guildhall
authorities presented Booth with the "freedom of the City of
London" and publicly eulogized his work.[29] Though scattered
incidents of opposition still occurred in the early years of this
century, both the public interference and official obstruction
largely came to an end during the late nineties, rather a notable
though long-delayed victory for freedom of assembly.

1. *The Times,* March 23, 1882.
2. Ibid., August 26, 1884.
3. *3 Hansard* CCLXIX (1882), 822.
4. Michael Pearson, *The £5 Virgins,* pp. 84 ff.; *3 Hansard* CCLXIX (1882), 820.
5. Hamilton Papers, B.M. Add. Mss 48647, p. 132, diary for January 22, 1888.

6. Gardiner, I, pp. 391, 410.

7. P.R.O., HO A5/A1775.

8. Great Britain, *Parliamentary Papers*, Vol. LIV (1882). "Return containing copies of any Correspondence which has passed between the Home Office and the Local Authorities of Basingstoke or other Places, with reference to the Suppression of Disturbances."

9. Mayor of Basingstoke to Home Office, April 2, 1881, P.R.O. HO 45/Box 9613/ A9275 "Basingstoke Correspondence."

10. Home Office to Stamford magistrates, October 4, 1881, published in *The Law Journal*, XVI (October 15, 1881), 480.

11. *3 Hansard* CCLXVIII (1882), 1271.

12. Ibid., CCLXIX (1882), 819; CCLXXII (1882), 447.

13. Beatty vs. Gillbanks, *Law Reports*, Q.B. 308; P.R.O. HO 45/A9275/17; See also HO 45/136764.

14. *3 Hansard* CCLXX (1882), 1413–1414.

15. Chief Constable to Mayor of Folkestone; Harcourt to Mayor of Folkestone, July 6, 1883, MEPOL 2/168.

16. *The Times*, September 9, 11, 1884.

17. Ibid., August 19, 1885.

18. *3 Hansard* CCCXXIV (1885), 258, 259.

19. P.R.O. HO 45/A9275/26.

20. *3 Hansard* CCCXIX (1887) 1528, 1807; CCCXXXVII (1889) 897-8, 1151, 1459.

21. *3 Hansard* CCCXIV (1887), 1765.

22. P.R.O. HO 45/A9275/38.

23. *3 Hansard* CCCLIII (1891), 1821–1822; CCCLIV (1891), 400.

24. 51 Vict., c. 279.

25. *4 Hansard*, II (1892), 497, 498; *3 Hansard* CCCXXVI (1888), 685.

26. *3 Hansard* CCCLIII (1891), 1821, 1822; Great Britain, *Parliamentary Papers*, Vol. LXV (1892), "Eastbourne Improvement Act, 1885 (Prosecutions for Open-air Services, etc.)."

27. 55 and 56 Vict., c. CXCIII.

28. *3 Hansard* CCCLV (1891), 1188; *4 Hansard*, I (1892), 1023, 1219; *Annual Register* (1892), II, 1,3,7.

29. *Annual Register* (1904), II, 15; (1905), 227; II, 28.

7

THE OUTDOOR DEMONSTRATION

The outdoor public meeting as a social phenomenon achieved a sort of apogee in late Victorian England. Weather permitting, Dickensian "Respectables" thronged the country's greens, parks, and commons to be harangued by a wide assortment of humanity going by the name of public lecturers.[1] Societies, leagues, and federations proliferated widely during the sixties, seventies, and eighties, each one anxious to enhance its influence and image by public demonstrations of popular support. It is no coincidence that the word "demonstration" in the sense of a meeting entered the English vocabulary in the eighteen-sixties. *The Times* complained in 1872 (9 August) that organizing demonstrations "...appears to be becoming a recognized branch of industry in this country." Causes such as that of the Tichborne Claimant would never have been sustained without the advertisement of continued demonstrations. Frequent appearances at public meetings made household words of such names as Charles Bradlaugh and John De Morgan. The public meeting may justifiably serve as one of the most characteristic symbols of Victorian society. By the 1880's Henry Matthews characterized its popularity as a national mania.

While the right of public meeting per se is an uncomplicated one guaranteed unequivocally in the Bill of Rights (1 William and Mary, Sess. 2, c2) and professed religiously by both major parties, the exercise of that right is fraught with most delicate legal niceties and practical ambiguities. Uniform guidelines proved illusive as the thin discriminating line between a dispersable and a legal gathering commonly blurred and on occasion vanished altogether. The police, in dynamic situations, faced the necessity of preserving order without escalating the risks of disorder by their own actions. The most difficult dilemmas landed in the Home Office, where the

Secretary was called upon to assess a wide range of sensibilities in dealing with them. Any prohibition supported by the Home Office was almost certain to elicit cries of violation of free speech with the accompanying danger of attracting even more sympathizers to whatever cause was at issue. Any signs of authorative leniency were apt to spur the demonstrators to greater risks. And, in addition, the Home Office, the police, and the organizers were acutely aware of the probability of rowdy elements being drawn to demonstrations for purposes having nothing to do with the intent of the organizers.

The optimistic response to demonstrations was, of course, to allow as much as possible and to "trust to the notorious good sense and loyalty of the great mass of the people," a view claimed by Gladstone repeatedly and implemented by Lord John Russell, Sir George Grey, and most of their Liberal Home Office successors.[2] On the other hand the paths of prohibition risked almost certain parliamentary and public allegations of tyranny. The Victorian Establishment, brought up on the classics, would easily cite Aristotle's comments on the tyrants' banning of public meetings (*Politics,* V. 11, 5, 6). Tory policies of the early nineteenth century had molded a Draconian impression in the public mind which later Conservative Home Secretaries did little to dispel. Sir James Graham's pronounced faith in the foolishness of the people of England and his expectation of the worst in them is well known. George Holyoake echoed the attitudes of most protest leaders in assuming the Tories were "always against public meetings as being unnecessary and inconvenient."[3]

We have seen the hard line Walpole attempted during the Hyde Park demonstrations of 1866 and 1867 and his successor, Hardy, continued along similar illiberal lines, his attitude no doubt greatly influenced by his confrontation with Fenianism. During the Fenian scare of 1867 he telegraphed the mayor of Liverpool:

> Apply to Orange leaders to stop their meeting and procession. Apply to Roman Catholic clergy to dissuade the people. Do everything in your power to prevent a collision and breach of the Peace. To do this you are justified in preventing meetings and stopping processions—let the people know they are stopped on these grounds. Magistrates are not to be bound by this but must exercize their own discretion—depending on Locality:

where meeting is held, numbers attending, force they have at their disposal, and other elements that cannot be known to the Secretary of State.[4]

That partisan considerations were not entirely absent may be indicated by Hardy's encouragement of a proposed loyalist demonstration at Bath at about the same time.[5] The severely regulatory
Parks Bill Hardy drafted had to be abandoned in the face of
lively liberal opposition and for some time the law remained
obscure. Some meetings were allowed; those of atheists, republicans and other obvious undesirables were not.

In December, 1868, the death of Sir Richard Mayne coincided
with the installation of a Liberal Government and brought about a
decidedly more tolerant official attitude toward public meetings.
The new Home Secretary, Henry Bruce, was an outspoken de-
fender not only of the right but the practice of free speech and
assembly. In the wake of the 1867 Hyde Park debacle, the status
of the law regarding public meetings there remained obscure.
But Bruce felt that Hyde Park assemblies had provided over the
years a beneficial, even tranquillizing, effect on the public mind.[6]
When in 1870 police removed a religious lecturer from the park,
Bruce rescinded the order by which the man had been arrested.
The order was that of Sir Richard Mayne, first given in 1862 to
prevent a Sunday "exciting speech" by Garibaldi.[7]

But even the liberal-minded Bruce seems not to have extended
the right of freedom of assembly to those who, in his estimation,
were wrongfully abusing it. Confronted with the prospect of
tumultuous Orange processions at Liverpool in 1869, he wrote to
the mayor of Liverpool: "If the justices have reason to believe the
procession may lead to a breach of the peace by reason of a collision being probable, they must cause an information to be laid
before them, on oath, to that effect, and then take means to stop
the procession by giving public notice, and applying to the heads
of the parties to stop it." If the procession still took place, "force
may be used to disperse it." These instructions were approved by
the Law Officers in 1873 so that they took the force of an L.O.O.[8]
Nor did Bruce's otherwise liberal stance extend to lecturers such
as Bradlaugh, whose republican meetings were frequently prohibited.

The greatest dilemma arose in the not unusual circumstance where hecklers and roughs not associated with the promoters instigated the disturbance. Justice John Karslake correctly assessed the problem in 1868: "Meetings and processions not themselves unlawful cannot legally be prevented simply because they may lead to breach of the peace....There is a great difficulty in dealing with these large meetings and processions where their purpose and objects are not avowedly of an unlawful manner."[9] Karslake's opinion was, in fact, so unpalatable that its fundamental principle was largely ignored by police and the Home Office until the 1880s.

The Parks Regulation Act of 1872 established for the first time uniform guidelines for all the Royal Parks and Gardens from sprawling Hyde Park to the Edinburgh Arboretum. "General Regulations" laid down basic policy for all the parks while "Rules" applied to some individual parks. The Rules for Hyde Park, Victoria Park, Battersea Park and Regent's Park expressly permitted public addresses of an orderly nature but only within precisely circumscribed open spaces of each park. Each of the parks remained under the supervision of the Board of Works whose chairman implemented the Rules and might add by-laws with the sanction of the Home Secretary. For the first time English statute law guaranteed open-air meetings in the Royal parks. During the 1870s most of the mammoth demonstrations were conducted in Hyde Park.

Actually much depended on the attitude of the Home Secretary. Occupying that office during the last six months of Gladstone's second ministry was Robert Lowe, nearing the end of a tempestuous public career. An albino whose eyes could tolerate virtually no light without grave discomfort, he was also the victim of extreme nearsightedness compounded by congenital defects. The Home Office was his last brief post as his sight gradually failed. Hardy noticed that Lowe "...does nothing at the H.O. indeed cannot physically read the papers."[10]

Lowe was succeeded by one of the ablest Home Secretaries of them all, Richard Cross. Born near Preston, Cross was descended from the old seventeenth-century family of Asshetons at Ashton-under-Lyne. At Rugby he learned from Arnold and made the lifetime friendship of Stanley (later the fifteenth Earl of

Derby); at Cambridge he rowed with the First Trinity Eight. He sat first as Member for Preston from 1857 to 1862, eventually relinquishing his seat for a banking partnership in Lancashire. In 1868 he defeated Gladstone in the new constituency of Southwest Lancashire. With no previous posts in government, no one was more surprised than Cross when Disraeli invited him to take the Home Office in 1874. "I was not prepared for such a signal mark of confidence and feel most deeply sensible of the responsibilities of the office. You may rest assured that no pains shall be spared on my part to justify your opinion." "What a jump up," was the startled response of Prince Leopold.[11] Actually the list Disraeli took to the Queen was one copied over by Correy, the original in Disraeli's hand showing Beach at the Home Office and Cross at the Board of Trade (Beach was instead placed as Secretary for Ireland).[12] During his six years at the Home Office, Cross framed much of the social legislation of Disraeli's last ministry and served again, also at the Home Office, under Salisbury, 1885–1886.

A reading of Cross' privately printed autobiography ("only intended for private circulation among members of my own family and very intimate friends") reveals a man proud of family lineage, conscious of titles, a man of some self-importance. At the Home Office this banker-businessman struck a firm business-like no-nonsense stance toward public order.

Over the years the Conservative Cross became one of the Queen's most trusted business advisors and confidants and she did not hesitate to voice her opinions and fears concerning public disorders. In 1876 Cross received the following note from Disraeli's private secretary: "Mr. Disraeli hears from the Queen that She wishes every possible enquiry to be made as to the state of public feeling in London, so that She may not be exposed to any annoyance on the occasion of Her going to open Parliament."[13]

A real problem soon developed concerning London's smaller commons and "open spaces" which attracted preachers and demagogues of every description. The Metropolitan Board of Works Act[14] placed these areas under the administration of the Metropolitan Board of Works which patrolled the commons with its own sentries. Subject to Home Office approval, the Metropolitan Board was also empowered to formulate by-laws for the regulation

Sir Richard Cross

of public meetings. Though the crowds drawn rarely approached the numbers who thronged Hyde Park, their proximity to residences surrounding the commons often provoked local neighborhood protest. In response to such circumstances at Clapham Common and elsewhere the Board, in 1877, authorized itself to prohibit at its discretion any public meeting on areas subject to its management and Cross routinely confirmed the by-law. Immediately upon the perhaps perfunctory approval of the by-law by the Home Secretary the Board proclaimed a blanket prohibition of "any public speech, lecture, sermon, or address of any kind or description whatsoever" without prior written permission. After an unsuccessful challenge by John De Morgan, the Board's policy remained in force for several years and there is no evidence that Cross objected.

Under Harcourt, however, there ensued a running battle between the Home Office and the Board over this question. In January of 1883 the Board issued a blanket prohibition of assemblies on Peckham Rye Common and the Lambeth Democratic Federation appealed to the Home Office. Harcourt suggested the Board reconsider and "...treat public meetings there as a matter of regulation and not of prohibition..." and the Board complied.[15]

Later the same year a similar case occurred in Rotherhithe where the Ratepayers Association had met in Southwark Park for Sunday meetings and had been arrested for violation of Board by-law. Harcourt's annoyance was thinly veiled:

> There is not a village or town in England, which has not some open space where gatherings of this kind can take place, and it would be intolerable if the population of London amounting to four millions of people, were destitute of such opportunities which are naturally and legitimately desired. Both Parliament and Crown have, in the administration of the parks under their control, evidenced their opinion that public meetings conducted in a peaceable and orderly manner constitute a proper and even useful employment of open spaces in the Metropolis. I think it would be a matter of regret if the Metropolitan Board took a different view of the open spaces which are under their management. Unnecessary repression of this character creates discontent and disturbance, and so far from tending to public order is calculated to provoke irritation and tumult.[16]

A second time the Board deferred to the wishes of the Home Secretary.

On the occasion of arrests of persons for reading the Scriptures on Sunday on Shepherd's Bush Common and the subsequent dismissal of such summonses in court, Harcourt again wrote in criticism of Board policy:

> The attempt to send people to prison for reading the Scriptures on Sunday upon Shepherd's Bush Common, appears to the Secretary of State to have been in every view of the case ill-judged....Prayer meetings are frequently held in different parts of the Metropolis, where perhaps if the Metropolitan Police were anxious to do so, they might be lawfully suppressed; but in the exercise of their discretion, the Police authorities judiciously refrain from interference, where no serious public inconvenience is created....It is not the part of wise administrators unnecessarily to interfere with the liberty already too much restricted, especially in places which, like the suburban commons, have heretofore been practically free![17]

The Board countered by alleging complaints from many houses "of a superior character" surrounding the common, and Harcourt replied that these houses already enjoyed advantages from proximity to the open space maintained at public expense. The Board then retorted that the Secretary's policy would mean allowing even anti-Christian speakers, a patently unconscionable course of action, as far as the Board was concerned. In addition, the Board claimed that Shepherd's Bush Common was not spacious enough to accommodate orderly assemblies and accused the Home Secretary of giving aid and comfort to those who "...set themselves deliberately to infringe the law."[18] Harcourt retaliated by vowing not to confirm any by-laws the Board might submit along these lines in the future and on this note of uncertainty the issue became dormant.

The dramatic increase in number and size of demonstrations and public meetings in the seventies and eighties posed renewed dilemmas for police authorities and ultimately the Home Office. The most troublesome were the demonstrations of the unemployed, the socialists, and religious preachers.

Street preaching as opposed to park meetings posed other peculiarly delicate problems for the police because of the additional features of neighborhood complaints and highway obstruction. When authorities interfered with speakers in response to resident complaints based only on noise disturbance, the speakers appealed on grounds of free speech and generally were upheld.

Police did prevent demonstrations adjacent to a surgery at the request of the doctor, and wherever obstruction to traffic was evident the law supported prohibition. Where there was no clear highway obstruction nor unusual circumstances, police generally allowed meetings to take place despite local expressions of annoyance, as in June, 1875, when police refused to interfere with a William Taylor, a Cabmen's Mission Hall speaker, at the corner of Liverpool Street in spite of repeated complaints by a resident, John Babcock.[19]

One of the most perplexing dilemmas of this kind occurred in the Limehouse district of East London in 1885. The area was a favorite of various radical groups, workingmen's associations, temperance societies, socialists and others. Through the summer police received numerous petitions from Limehouse inhabitants complaining of the "nuisance" of these speakers. After repeated warnings police arrested two temperance orators and a third who allegedly incited the mob to rescue the others, followed by sporadic arrests in August and September, including those of Social Democratic Federation speakers Henry Champion and Jack Williams. All of the arrests took place on Sundays in Dodd Street and the SDF contended no obstruction occurred because of the total absence of traffic in Dodd Street at the times in question.[20]

The arrests but scotched the snake and led to the opposite of their intended effect. In retaliation a number of the threatened groups planned an even larger protest rally in Dodd Street for Sunday, September 20. By noon, one thousand demonstrators thronged the area. As the speakers began an impromptu meeting seven arrests were made by constables in spite of a good deal of mob interference. The charges were "open-air preaching and causing a crowd to assemble in Dodd Street, thereby causing an obstruction and annoyance to the inhabitants." At Thames Police Court Magistrate Saunders discharged one, sentenced two to two months hard labor and five others to 40 shillings or one month. Mr. Saunders allowed himself to argue with the defendants during the trial prompting many complaints on the part of spectators. As the sentences were announced an outraged William Morris hissed and shouted, "shame" again and again and scuffled with restraining officers barely escaping arrest himself. It was at this point the attention of the Home Secretary was first called to the case. Cross was again back in the Home Office following the Conservative victory of 1885 and went on record as regretting such police interference and asked Saunders for a report. Saunders justified his conduct to the Home Office later that week blaming the "very unruly and most unbecoming behavior of the defendants which induced me to admonish them."[21] The Bishop of Bedford wrote to Cross that the sentences seem excessive, "perilous" in that "they are exciting a spirit of wrath and indignation which it may be hard to quench and which may lead to disastrous consequences."[22] Professor E.P. Beesly of the London Positivist Society denounced both the police arrests and the magistrate's reprehensible conduct in entering into debates with the defendants. "He has made it plain that what he desired to put down was not street obstructionism but the preaching of socialism."[23]

The arrests tended to unify the various groups under the banner of freedom of public meeting, a pose the *Morning Post* derided as nonsense.[24] General press coverage favored the police action. During the ensuing week police suggestions that the speakers move their Sunday gatherings to a vacant lot not a quarter mile from Dodd Street were scorned by the organizers who called for an even larger protest rally for the following Sunday. The police warned the Home Office of the prospects of controlling a meeting of "gigantic proportions." The position of the Metropolitan force was that the legality of the arrests had been upheld in court and that any backing down would be seen as a fatal sign of weakness, a position put very persuasively by both Commissioner Monro and his assistant (Bruce) in personal visits to the Home Office.[25] Both Cross and Police Superintendent Henderson were out of town. A critical meeting took place at the Home Office on Thursday the 24th. Under-Secretary Pemberton held a face-to-face discussion between Aveling, who represented the protest organizers, and Bruce and Monro of the Metropolitan force. Aveling was conciliatory and gave assurances that the Sunday rally would not only be orderly, but that, if conceded, it would be the last one in Dodd Street. Bruce and Monro remained adamant, urging on the Home Office an absolute prohibition enforced by the presence of an overwhelming show of police including cavalry, if necessary. No common ground was found and Pemberton, after the meeting ended in impasse, telegraphed Cross that "the position is scarcely satisfactory."[26]

Bruce returned to the Home Office Friday bearing a neighborhood petition strongly supportive of the police position. Pemberton telegraphed Cross: "The Commissioners are of the opinion that to allow a meeting in Dodd Street now...would be a confession that the Police and magistrates were wrong and would have a disastrous effect." Henderson was sent for. The police were exerting every pressure on the Home Office for support.

In the end Cross decided against the police proposal. The following letters and telegram suggest strongly that the imminent election weighed heavily in the Home Secretary's decision. On the 25th he wrote:

> ...if the Police are judicious there ought to be no difficulty...Please see to this for it is very important. There can be no doubt that as the election approaches these people will assert their right to proclaim their views, a right which I conclude is undeniable and the difficulty will be to see that as little public inconvenience takes place as possible. But if the Police were to be injudicious the issue would at once be changed and serious riots might be the result....Sir Edmund Henderson must be in town. If he is not send for him. The greatest prudence and tact will be necessary.

And again the same day:

> Since writing the above I have received the enclosed letter from the Bishop of Bedford—no one knows the East End people better than he does. And I have no fancy myself for anything like a blaze. I have certainly no intention whatever of giving the mob anything like grounds for saying that on the eve of an election freedom of speech is denied to which I believe them entitled. I see in the papers that Dodd Street is only a street of warehouses and worn down tenant houses. Anyhow I quite expect to hear from you that the police have been able to arrange matters somehow. In fact they *must* do it. So you may tell them.

By telegraph on the 25th:

> My minute of last night will show that I do not take quite the same view as the police. I wish the case had been before me last week but from your minute I see no difficulty. Their proposal is that the meeting is to be conducted in an orderly manner and I presume so as to hinder traffic as little as possible so let it be arranged in some way or other as satisfactorily as possible. As the case is at present presented to me I could not sanction the notices [of prohibition]. I think the proposed course [of the police] would only lead into further and greater difficulties whereas at present this other course is open without loss of dignity to the police.[27]

Thus the police were overruled.

Upon returning to London on Saturday, Henderson reluctantly gave notice that the police would not interfere with the meeting as long as there was no disorder or obstruction to traffic. In return the organizers labored feverishly to guarantee the promised order. Stewards were assigned to accompany each contingent of marchers from various quarters of London. Each procession was timed to converge on Dodd Street at noon. As the lead carriage arrived at Dodd Street, Bateman, a well-known socialist, urged the crowds not to disgrace the movement by disturbance. The stewards were careful to keep open all traffic lanes and to give police no cause to interfere. Placards read: "Free Speech! Fellow men, let our motto be Peace, Right and Resistance, Sunday after Sunday, until this struggle shall end." The police stood round listening to speeches by G.B. Shaw, Henry Hyndman, the Reverend Stewart Headlam and others. A telegram was read from the Chicago Socialist Working Men's Association: "Hurrah for the London Revolution! Vive la Revolution." Except for a few scattered liberty caps and some exaggerated language, the whole affair passed off rather quietly and respectably. Certainly it constituted no revolution. Hyndman considered it a "famous victory," the police felt betrayed, and the *Daily Telegraph* (Conservative) labeled the government's policy "a crushing defeat."[28]

One of the most popular speakers at Dodd Street that Sunday of 1885 was a twenty-six-year-old apprentice engineer (at the time unemployed) who hailed the "bloodless revolution that had taken place that day in East London on behalf of the workers of the world." John Burns was unquestionably one of the most powerful and fiery of the many street orators of the 1880s. One of eighteen children of a family deserted by the father and whose mother was illiterate, he left home and school at the age of ten to find work as an apprentice engineer. In and out of work the next several years of his life, educated at night school, young Burns found himself drawn more and more to the life of a street agitator: "I myself, with my wife, have frequently left home at 3 and 4 o'clock in the morning, winter and summer; tramped to the docks, made speeches at three different gates, and returned to begin my day's work in the West End at 7 or 8 o'clock. I have done this for weeks and months together."[29] In 1884 Burns joined Hyndman in the Social Democratic Federation and from that time on was involved in almost every socialist and radical agitation

John Burns

in London throughout the eighties. He played a leading part in the unemployed demonstrations of the mid-eighties, and was the one individual most responsible for circumstances which led to the Pall Mall affair of February 8, 1886, or, as it was commonly styled in the popular press of the day, "Black Monday."

1. For a partial list of public demonstrations from the 1860s to the 1880s see *PP*, XXXIV (1886), C. 4665, Appendix VII, p. 99.

2. The quoted phrase is Gladstone's: *3 Hansard* CCV (1871), 574.5. Stanley Baldwin echoed the same sentiment in 1926. See also F.C. Mather, *Public Order in the Age of the Chartists*, pp. 40-44, and Spencer Walpole, *The Life of Lord John Russell*, I, p. 316.

3. Graham, Home Secretary 1841-1846, had advocated the suppression of all large public meetings regardless of their character. H.O. to Lyttelton dated August 19, 1842. HO 41/17. George Holyoake, *Sixty Years of an Agitator's Life*, II, p. 186.

4. Hardy to Mayor of Liverpool, December 13, 1867; P.R.O. HO 41/21/103. This telegram followed a personal consultation with the Attorney General (Sir John Karslake) at the Home Office.

5. Hardy to Mayor of Bath, December 25, 1867; P.R.O. HO 41/21/159.

6. *Gladstone Papers*, Bruce to Gladstone, March 1, 1872, B.M. Add. Mss. 44087 f. 46.

7. "Meetings in Hyde Park, or any park in the Metropolis.—The meetings for the purpose of delivering or hearing speeches, or for the public discussion of popular and exciting topics, are not to be allowed on Sundays in any of the parks." HO 45/A43210/2/14.

8. July 12, 1873; HO 45/136764.

9. June 3, 1868, HO 45/O.S./8174 (L.O.O. #179).

10. Hardy to Cairns, November 21, 1873, Cairns Papers, P.R.O. 30/51/7.

11. Cross to Disraeli, February 19, 1874, Hughenden Papers, B/XII/A/13; Price to Cross, February 24, 1874, Cross Papers, B.M. Add. Mss. 51270 f. 198.

12. Hughenden Papers, B/XII/A/1.

13. Corry to Cross, January 11, 1876, Cross Papers, B.M. Add. Mss. 51271.

14. 40 Vict., c. 8 (1877), extended by 45 Vict., c. 56. See "Public Meetings in the Metropolis" (1886), HO 45/A43210/2.

15. HO 45/A19155.

16. Harcourt to Chairman of Metropolitan Board of Works, August 1883, HO 45/12731/17.

17. HO 45/A43210/2/23-24.

18. Metropolitan Board of Works to Harcourt, December 12, 1884, HO 45/A 31066/7.

19. P.R.O. MEPOL 2/168.

20. P.R.O. HO 45/X7215. See Henry Hyndman, *Record of an Adventurous Life*, p. 387.

21. Saunders to Cross, September 25, 1885, HO 45/X7215/13.

22. Bishop of Bedford to Cross, September 23, 1885, HO 45/X7215/16.

23. Beesley to Cross, September 25, 1885, HO 45/X7215.
24. *Morning Post,* September 21, 1885.
25. HO 45/X7215/15.
26. Pemberton to Cross, September 24, 1885, HO 45/X7215/18.
27. Cross to Pemberton, September 24, 25, 1885, HO 45/X7215/18.
28. *Daily Telegraph,* September 28, 1885.
29. Quoted in G.H. Knott, *Mr. John Burns, M.P.,* p. 37.

8

THE PALL MALL AFFAIR-
ANATOMY OF A RIOT

The Pall Mall Affair of 1866 originated in the long-standing rivalry of the socialists and the Fair Trade movement for the blessing and support of English labor. The Fair Trade movement was an anti-socialist response to the hard times of the mid-1880s. It enjoyed slight chance of enduring success, but wielded considerable influence during the worst of the depression years. The Fair Traders laid the blame for the economic malaise on "unfair" foreign competition and argued for the restoration of tariff protection. The movement was buttressed by many Conservatives and later by Liberal manufacturers and was always alive to the prospects of capturing a segment of the working class. It was for this purpose that the Fair Traders sponsored the London United Workmen's Committee which orchestrated rallies and demonstrations in the mid-eighties geared to the unemployed.

Arch-rivals of the Fair Traders for the sympathy of the working classes were the new socialist bodies. The Democratic Federation had been founded in 1881 by Henry Hyndman, a middle-class, Marxist-influenced journalist. In 1884 G.B. Shaw, Sidney and Beatrice Webb and others launched the Fabian Society and later that year William Morris dropped out of Hyndman's renamed Social Democratic Federation to found the Socialist League. These groups viewed the Fair Traders as traitors to the laboring classes, bogus imposters, puppets of the capitalists. As both competed for the support of the unemployed, rival heckling gave way to physical disruption and several collisions between the two groups had already occurred. Burns regarded the Fair Traders as "the most infamous scoundrels that ever wore boot-leather in the streets of London," parasites on the labor movement.[1] Bradlaugh made public a widely-believed charge that leading Conservatives, in-

cluding the prime minister himself, had donated funds to sponsor
the Fair Traders' Trafalgar Square agitations. Bradlaugh was later
to face libel action on this account.

It is clear that it was the Fair Traders who first planned a mass
demonstration of and for the unemployed on the 8th of February
in Trafalgar Square. They prepared printed placards (see illustration) advertising their program schedule. Their plan was that contingents of unemployed would gather at various staging areas and
march toward Trafalgar Square by designated routes in order to
converge on the square simultaneously, shortly before 3 o'clock.

Burns openly boasted that he and the Social Democratic Federation had conspired to sabotage the Fair Traders' meeting:
"Steal the pitch before they arrive," as Burns put it. "I'm to bell
the cat and be chairman."[2] The plan was to dish the Fair Traders
by capturing their audience or by obstructing the Fair Traders'
resolutions by moving rival amendments, heckling, and as a last
resort, physical disruption. Involved in the plot along with Burns
were Hyndman, the proletarian Jack Williams, and Henry Hyde
Champion. The latter was the son of a Major-General, an artillery
officer who had abandoned a commission in the army to become
sub-editor of *The Nineteenth Century*.

Somehow the Fair Traders got wind of the socialists' subversion
intentions and conveyed this information to the police. In an
interview on February 3 the committee met with Chief Inspector
Cutbush; they advised him that if the SDF should try to interfere with their meeting there probably would be a disturbance and
they suggested extra police precautions to augment their own
force of five hundred Stewards and fifty Marshals.

On the 5th of February Henderson reviewed police preparations
with Cross, who reiterated the routine caution that an ample force
be deployed, especially in view of the possibility of a collision.
This was Cross' last day at the Home Office. Salisbury had already
resigned on January 27th, and Gladstone was at the very time
forming a new cabinet. The Irish question was paramount in
government circles. Gladstone's son, Herbert, had just leaked
prematurely his father's closet conversion to Home Rule, and the
Liberal Unionists were fast abandoning the Grand Old Man. Gladstone was preoccupied the entire weekend with cabinet-making.

Dilke was, of course, about to face divorce court and had to be dropped from consideration. Goschen and Hartington refused all posts, while Chamberlain took the presidency of the Local Government Board only to resign the following month. Gladstone wished Harcourt back at the Home Office, but the "Old Gladiator" had no desire to return to "the detested Home Office." Following personal consultation with Gladstone, Harcourt happily escaped to the Chancellorship of the Exchequer. The Home Office at length went to Childers, whom Gladstone had intended originally for the War Office.

H. (Hugh) C.E. Childers, the same age as Harcourt, was also born at York, the son of a Yorkshire clergyman. An experienced administrator in colonial affairs, he had held many different posts in Gladstone's cabinets, "without whom it was one of Mr. Gladstone's foibles to think that no Liberal Cabinet was adequately equipped," according to Asquith.[3] He attended Oxford, graduated from Cambridge, studied at Lincoln's Inn for a short period, although he was never called to the bar. He was, in fact, the only Home Secretary of this period who was not a barrister. As Secretary for War he had implemented some of the most far-reaching of Cardwell's reforms, but he earned the hearty dislike of the Queen and the Duke of Cambridge in so doing. The Queen was also displeased by his seemingly cavalier attitude toward the dangers of radical and socialist agitations.

Both his private and public life were overshadowed by misfortune. His father had died when he was barely four; the death of a son in the foundering of the *Captain* in 1870 left him grief-stricken and his health broke down forcing retirement. The sudden death of his wife in 1875 again forced a temporary withdrawal from public life. Plagued by continuing family problems, Childers accepted the unwanted Home Office at a most unpropitious moment.

Henderson distinctly recalled that at the Friday meeting neither he nor the out-going Cross took a particularly ominous view of the prospects due to the customary orderliness which had come to characterize London demonstrations in the decade. Later in the day Henderson met with Assistant Commissioner Pearson and Chief Inspector Cutbush, head of the Executive Branch, and it

H.C.E. Childers

was agreed to field a force of 260 police reserves in addition to the routine patrols in view of the possible collision.

Monday was "clear and frosty," ideal for the kind of demonstration and counter-demonstration planned by the rival groups. During the morning Henderson increased the reserve force to five hundred (plus officers). "We are more responsible than ever, just now, because there is really virtually no Secretary of State; and we will have plenty of men."[4]

Childers arrived at the Home Office for the first time close to noon on Monday. Crowds had already begun to gather nearby in the square. Childers sent for Henderson and Pearson to enquire whether adequate forces had been assigned in view of the planned counter-demonstrations and the two gave assurances that the forces deployed and in reserve would be sufficient for any contingency.

Long experience seemed to justify the adequacy of the precautions taken although many of the five hundred constables Henderson had called up for reserve duty, fifty from each Division, had been on duty the night before and were liable to go on duty again the night after. One hundred were deployed to St. George's Barracks adjacent to the square itself, sixty to King Street Station to protect the Houses of Parliament, twenty to Vine Street Station between Regent Street and Piccadilly, and the remaining 320 to Scotland Yard within easy access to Trafalgar Square. No mounted police were commonly used for crowd control on these occasions. In charge of these forces were fifty sergeants, ten inspectors, and three District superintendents, Hume, Walker, and Dunlop. Assistant Commissioner Monro, in charge of C.I.D. (Criminal Investigation Department) sent four plainclothes detectives to the square under Chief Inspector Shore. They were to mingle with the crowd, coming back with reports to Monro every fifteen to twenty minutes. Chief Inspector Cutbush manned the Scotland Yard Telegraph, which at the time linked headquarters to almost every London police station.

Overall command of the "police arrangements" in Trafalgar Square itself was given to its District Superintendent, Robert Walker. He received no special instructions concerning the demonstration, no intimation of the probable counter-demonstration. He had not had a hand in planning the deployment of the reserves and he learned of his duty in the square only routinely that same morning. Walker was seventy-four years of age. He would not appear on the scene until about 2:30 in the afternoon.

Dunlop was first in the square with fifty of his own reserves from Division A (King Street Station). He arrived at one o.clock and deployed thirty of his men around Nelson's Column and twenty in ten double patrols around the outskirts of the crowd, which had already increased to about fifteen to twenty thousand. W.T. Stead, having just completed a three-month sentence on his famous morals conviction, was there. But there were few other top-hatters. Most of the crowd were undoubtedly the unemployed.

Burns and the other socialists arrived in the square at about 1:30 and were instantly acclaimed by the crowd. They approached Nelson's Column, which was surrounded by Dunlop's police. According to Burns, he and Champion were forcibly hoisted by the mob onto the plinth of the monument and after consultation with Superintendent Dunlop they were allowed to make short speeches:

> Our meeting at the Nelson Column was satisfactorily conducted. Quietness and order prevailed. After speaking I called on several whom I recognized in the crowd, and resolutions were submitted to about 20,000 persons, for by this time the crowd had considerably augmented. No damage was done. There was no conflict with the police. We avoided that, as Superintendent Dunlop admits.[5]

Burns' version of what happened differed considerably from Dunlop's recollection under oath:

> They were almost going at the double across the Square, making, as I could see, for the column. I said to my inspector, 'They are on us.' My line was immediately broken; it was a very thin one at that time. They mounted up on all quarters; the man in the blue serge suit being very conspicuous. The crowd, in spite of our endeavour to keep them back, pressed us very closely against the column. So much so, that I could hardly get breath, and my men were hard put to it. I said 'Stick to it lads, we will get help presently, do not let us be beaten by them.' I sent one of the constables to Scotland Yard for help immediately. I saw Burns was going to speak, and I then caught him by the leg, and I said 'Look here, young gentleman, you or I must be master here; we cannot have any speaking here.' He said, 'Are you in charge of the police.' I said, 'Never you mind what I am. I am in uniform, and that is enough for you.' He said, 'Just give me five or six minutes and there shall be no row. I will clear off in a minute.' Though I do not like temporising with men like that, yet I thought discretion was the better part

of valour, and I knew that I had no help, and that they had broken my line, and that I must, therefore, do the best I could, and I said, 'Make your speech as short as you can,' and he commenced making a short speech. In a few minutes some one handed him up a small red flag like a railway flag. I do not know who it was, but it was some poor fellow with hardly a shoe to his foot; he waved it round his head and said, 'Three cheers for the Socialistic Republic.'[6]

After Burns dismounted from the pedestal, Dunlop's augmented force reclaimed the monument and maintained a strong protective cordon for the rest of the afternoon.

Dunlop later testified that he considered the crowd a rougher one than was usual at such meetings. One of his sergeants was asked at the inquiry: "Are you in the habit, when you are on duty under such circumstances as you were in on Monday last, of being in such a practically powerless condition as to be buffeted about and carried off your legs and tossed and driven about by the crowd as you seem to have been?—No, I have never been before in such a crowd as what it was on Monday." Dunlop, himself, was thrown to the ground "probably a dozen times" near Nelson's Column that afternoon, and so were many of his men (Q2304).

At about three o'clock the Fair Traders and their workers' delegations arrived, accompanied by their Stewards and Marshals, and mounted their platforms on the north side of the square. Walker and most other witnesses later verified that the Fair Traders conducted a very orderly meeting, urged the support of labor for protectionism and deprecated violence in any form.

At this point Champion and Burns, the latter still brandishing the red flag, made their way through the dense crowd toward the Fair Traders at the northern side of the square. Joined now by Hyndman and Williams, the four clambered up onto the balustrade of the National Galley. Burgess described the scene which ensued:

> Burns, in opening the meeting, declared that he and his friends of the Revolutionary Social Democratic League were not there to oppose the agitation for the unemployed, but they were there to prevent the people being made the tools of the paid agitators who were working in the interests of the Fair Trade League.
>
> He went on to denounce the House of Commons as composed of capitalists who had fattened on the labour of the working men, and in this category he included landlords, railway directors, and employers, who, he said, were no more likely to legislate in the interests of the working men than were the wolves to labour for the lambs.

To hang these people, he said, would be to waste good rope, and as no good to the people was to be expected from these 'representatives,' there must be a revolution to alter the present state of things.

The people who were out of work, he continued, did not want relief, but justice. From whom should they get justice? From such as the Duke of Westminister and his class, or the capitalists in the House of Commons and their class?

No relief or justice would come from them.

The working men had now the vote conferred upon them. What for? To turn one party out and put the other in? Were they going to be content with that while their wives and children wanted food?

When the people of France demanded food, the rich laughed at those they called the 'men in blouses,' but the heads of those who laughed soon decorated the lamp-posts.

Here the leaders of the Revolutionary Democratic League wanted to settle affairs peaceably if they could; but if not, they would not shrink from revolution.[7]

Champion, Williams and Hyndman followed Burns in the socialist counterdemonstration. Hyndman pointed toward club-land in Pall Mall: "Look at those clubs. What did the members of those clubs care for their distress? Where were the Members of Parliament that day? They were sitting comfortably in their clubs, not caring a straw whether the people starved or not. The only hope left lay in revolution." Still clinging to the balustrade, Burns shouted that the next time the unemployed met "it would be to go and sack the bakers' shops in the West End of London. They had had too much talk....The next time they met it would not be to speak, but to take the wealth of which they had been robbed," particularly unfortunate language in view of what was about to transpire. Burns pointed to the Fair Traders and vilified their leaders as paid agitators who battened on the poverty of the poor.[8] At about this juncture Burns' sufficiently inflamed followers made a rush at the Fair Traders' platforms, overturned them, and a brief mêlée ensued. After the successful attack on the platforms, a more or less spontaneous suggestion was made to march through the West End, prompted perhaps by the inflammatory language employed by the socialist orators. Apparently unnoticed by the police, a sizable crowd broke off from the mass and disappeared into Pall Mall, led by Champion, Williams, Burns with his red flag or handkerchief, and Hyndman in his incongruous top hat.

Burns was later lionized by radical circles as the "Man With the Red Flag." Among Burns' papers in the British Museum are his

Demonstration of Unemployed Workmen

Trafalgar Square, Monday, Feb 8th. at 3 p.m.

PROGRAMME OF ROUTE.

1.—The Men from South London will assemble and March in procession from the Obelisk, near the Surrey Theatre, at 2 p.m. and proceed by way of Blackfriars, Fleet Street, Strand, to Trafalgar Square.

2.—The Men from East London will assemble and March in procession from Mile End Waste, at 1-30 p.m., by way of Whitechapel Road, through the City, Cheapside, St. Paul's Churchyard, Fleet Street, to Trafalgar Square.

3.—The Men from the Northern and East Central portions of London will assemble on Clerkenwell Green, and March at 2 p.m., by way of Farringdon Road, Charterhouse Street, High Holborn, down St. Andrew's Street, St. Martin's Lane, to Trafalgar Square.

4.—Men from the South-West, West Central and West parts of the Metropolis, should make their way towards Trafalgar Square, reaching there not later than 2-45 p.m.

There will be 500 Stewards, under 50 Marshals, each one of whom will have charge of 10 Stewards; these will be distinguished by wearing on their left breast a small piece of Green Ribbon, the Committee having taken these steps for the purpose of assisting the Police in preserving order.

At No. 1 PLATFORM,

MR. PATRICK KENNY,

General Secretary of the General Labourer's Amalgamated Union, will preside.

At No. 2 PLATFORM,

MR. FREDK. WIGINGTON,

General Secretary of the Amalgamated Watermen and Lightermen's Society, will preside.

At No. 3 PLATFORM,

CAPTAIN THOMAS LEMON,

President of the British Seamen's Society, will preside.

WORKING MEN from all parts of London, attend this Demonstration in your Thousands—demonstrate peaceably—and show the Government and the public that the time has come when the wretched condition of our Industrial Classes should be at once grappled with, and their sufferings relieved.

BE MODERATE. BE WISE. BE RESOLUTE.

By Order.
THE LONDON UNITED WORKMEN'S COMMITTEE,
CENTRAL CLUB HOUSE, "ROSE" TAVERN, OLD BAILEY, E.C.

A. Parkes, Trades Union Printer, 226, Southwark Bridge Road, S.E.

"Demonstration of Unemployed Workmen" Meeting Notice

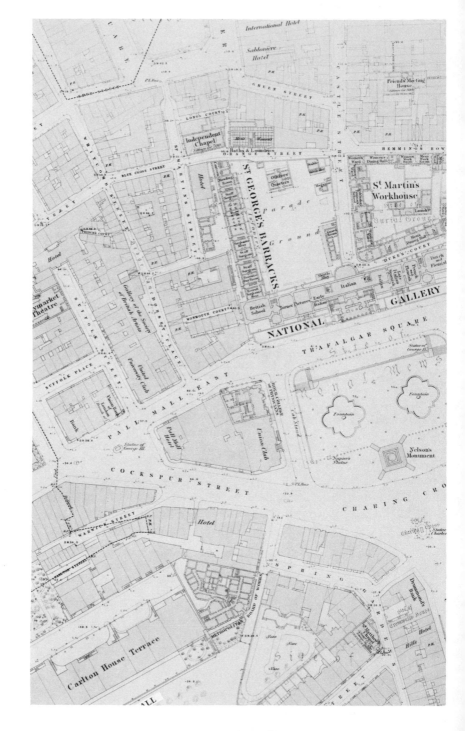

Map of Trafalgar Square

notes for a never-published autobiography in which he admitted the "red flag" was the merest coincidence. He recalled a hurried conversation with a police inspector just before his departure for Hyde Park:

> The Police Inspector said to me 'What are you going to do now?'
> I said: 'I am going to march the men along Pall Mall to HP Corner and disperse them there.'
> 'Very good' he said 'I'll make arrangements, but how shall we be able to tell where you are if we want to speak to you'?
> 'I'll tell you what I'll do' I said, 'I'll tie a handkerchief on the end of my stick like a flag and wherever you see that you'll know where to find me".
> I had only a white pocket hankerchief so I turned round to the crowd and said 'Can any one lend me a hankerchief' A navvy produced a big red handkerchief from his pocker and I tied that to my stick and was carried along shoulder-high by the crowd. There was no premeditation about it but that was the thing the papers seized upon and I became known as "The Man With the Red Flag."[9]

There is no substantiation of this recollection which entails several suspect features, but Burns was known on other occasions not to deny himself the embellishment of a good story.

Following his briefing given at the Home Office, Henderson went directly to Trafalgar Square to mingle in the crowds throughout the afternoon. He was in plain clothes and seems to have been a bit swallowed up in the crush. He could not manage to get close enough to hear any of the speakers, he never saw a man with a red flag, he missed the overturning of the Fair Traders' platforms, and he did not notice the departure of the Pall Mall crowd. During a brief respite at Scotland Yard he remarked to Pearson that "it was the quietest meeting he had seen for a long time."[10] If there was to be any trouble, he anticipated it would take place in the square.

The seventy-four year old Walker, also in plain clothes and top hat, arrived on the scene at about 2:30 when the square was already jammed with demonstrators and on-lookers. For a while he directed traffic on the east side of the square. Although he later maintained "I was everywhere," Henderson never saw him once the whole afternoon and Dunlop could recall not one order given by Walker. "He was lost in the crowd. It would have been impossible to find him." During a brief rest at the Yard, Walker admitted to Pearson he had gotten "very much jammed up in the crowd." He did not remember a man with a red flag, but did see the overturning of the speakers' platforms: "Pieces of wood, and seemingly a coat, began to fly backwards and forwards, and I made an effort to get through to find out the cause, but the pressure when fairly in was beyond what I could stand, and with difficulty got back," not before four pickpockets emptied all his pockets. "One was utterly powerless to act for one's self, every man around being probably a thief, and this was their harvest." Walker felt responsibility only for activity in the square itself. "My duties were so onerous in Trafalgar Square that looking to the four corners of it was beyond my power."[11] He, too, could not recall the departure of any sizable segment of the crowd in the direction of Pall Mall. Officially in charge of the entire police operation, Walker seems to have spent the afternoon a victim adrift in the very maelstrom he was supposed to control. At about 2:30 Hume ordered the steps of the National Gallery cleared and the gates secured for the day. The attention of all police authorities was thus concentrated almost exclusively on the crowd in the square itself. They were to remain oblivious to the rampage begun elsewhere until it was too late.

Pall Mall was one of London's most venerable avenues. It was named after a seventeenth-century game played here. Pepys mentions "Pail Mail" in 1660. Gainsborough lived here in the eighteenth century. The spacious avenue became, in the nineteenth century, the center of London club-land, lined on either side by the most prestigious gentlemen's clubs of the period.

A single stone shattered a window at a wine merchant's near the United Service Club at 3:50, the time pinpointed by the merchant himself. The long march of the Pall Mall mob had commenced. Led by Burns, the crowd pressed by the Athenaeum with its sixty thousand volume library where Faraday was once honorary secretary, continued on past the sentry at the Guard's Monument, the Travelers' Club, the Farncsc facade of the Reform Club, until it reached the Carlton, the chief Conservative club-house of the Metropolis. Its broad mid-century Italian facade cradled an exclusive membership never to exceed 1,600 and who were eager to pay £ 30 fee plus an annual ten guineas. According to Burns:

> What started the trouble was the sight of a Member of the Carlton
> Club standing at the window and putting his fingers to his nose as the

procession passed. This infuriated the men who had everything at stake. Then there were some servant girls at the upper windows who threw some crusts or match-boxes into the crowd. The men simply went mad. They made a rush for the door of the Club. They hurled their sticks at the windows. Anything they could find to fling they flung. They even tore the war medals off their breasts for missiles. Windows were broken all along Pall Mall. Next day there was a stream of men calling at the Club to ask for their medals to be returned. Most of them got them.[12]

The secretary of the Carlton estimated the numbers of the crowd at between two and three thousand and that they stopped about twenty minutes in front. "When they first arrived, they were giving cheers, until some man who got on the balustrading took out a red handkerchief or flag, and began addressing them; and three or four minutes after he had done addressing them, they began to throw at the other windows." Stones were readily available in Pall Mall due to construction work in progress. Two club-men were robbed in the street. There was a police officer on duty outside the War Office and a telephone communication inside, the only one available in the neighborhood. Although only one hundred fifty yards from the Carlton, this officer claimed never to have seen any damage worth reporting, and he, of course, took no action alone since the War Office itself was not under attack. Burns claimed that he was at length able to quell the stoning at the Carlton and the crowd resumed its progress toward Hyde Park.

Back in the square at about the same time, the main meeting was breaking up and the police were preoccupied by the movements of the crowd as it began to disperse. Henderson, at the foot of Nelson's Column with Dunlop, recalled only a dense mass of people: "they began to go away, and they went away." As expected, most of the crowds seemed to be dispersing as usual toward their homes in the East End. Almost as an idle superfluous precaution, however, Henderson thought some might drift into Pall Mall, and so ordered Dunlop to send the remaining reserves in St. George's Barracks down to Pall Mall, but at the time he was oblivious of the significance of his action.

The constable Dunlop chose to carry the fateful message was an "old and intelligent" constable, William Hull, an eight-year veteran on the force. Actually, Dunlop's "old" constable was only thirty-five years of age. Half-running and half-walking, Hull fought his way through the surging mob to the barracks only to instruct

Hume to take his reserve force to The Mall, instead of Pall Mall (See map. p. 112). Like Cardigan at the tragic battlefield of Bala-clava, Hume never questioned the orders, but set out immediately for The Mall where, quite naturally, he assumed he was to protect Buckingham Palace. Due to the congestion Hume sent out his one hundred men not in marching order, but in broken ranks with in-structions to reassemble at the Duke of York's steps. Some chose a route through the Warwick Mews, and some cross Pall Mall itself; it was later established that they missed the mob by only ten to twenty minutes. As they were counted off at the steps, the sentry there at the Guard's Monument reported having seen a crowd in Pall Mall but no disorder. Hume nevertheless marched his force quickly up The Mall, leaving fifty at Marlborough House standing at ease with their backs to the railings of St. James Park, and tak-ing the other half all the way to the Palace where he stationed them along the railings of the Palace, prepared for any emergency.

At about the same time Henderson sent (or thought he had sent) protective forces into Pall Mall, Inspector Shore learned from one of his plainclothesmen in the square that some crowds had drifted off into Pall Mall. Shore looked for Walker, was unable to locate him, and ran to Scotland Yard "very breathless" to report to Monro. His chief in the C.I.D. was at that moment at the Home Office paying a courtesy call upon Childers. Pearson suggested Shore try again to find Walker in the square, so Shore raced back to the square but "Mr. Walker is a man whom you would not find unless you ran close against him in a crowd. He is not a tall man." Despairing of ever locating Walker, Shore ran back a second time to the Yard where Cutbush authorized him to go to St. George's Barracks and send Hume and the reserves into Pall Mall. Upon ar-riving at the barracks, Shore discovered that the reserves had al-ready left and assumed they had gone to Pall Mall. He himself passed Pall Mall, noticed the damage to the Carlton and retraced his steps a third time to Scotland Yard to report the damage to Pearson. By this time it was 4:30. Both Henderson and Pearson had ordered reserves to Pall Mall after the damage had been done and neither became aware at the time that the force had been misdirected to The Mall and Buckingham Palace. Inexplicably, Shore failed to attach any significance to the fact that when he had visited Pall Mall no police reserves were there as he should have expected. Pearson spent the next hour at Scotland Yard, an hour that in retrospect "appears to me really like a dream. I heard absolutely nothing from 4 o'clock to 5:05."[13]

Oblivious to the near interception, Burns and the socialists, with their unemployed in tow, continued their procession unimpeded. From time to time they indulged in indiscriminate stoning, aware of no distinctions between clubs. The Reform Club, the Beaconsfield and the Marlborough escaped damage, but the Service Club and Brooks's were badly stoned. White's and Boodles, both extremely aristocratic, were ignored while the radical Devonshire suffered much damage. One of the most severely stoned was the New University Club from which Hyndman had recently been expelled for wrong (socialist) ideas, the merest coincidence according to him.

At the bottom of St. James Street the mob was confronted by contemptuous jeering from the Thatched House and responded again with volleys of stones. A single intrepid constable, on Fixed Point routine duty on the corner, attempted an arrest of one of the stone-throwers, but he was instantly knocked down and his prisoner escaped. Lone sentries at St. James Palace and Marlborough House also witnessed the attack on the Thatched House, but "being on special duty, they did not like to leave their post."

Leading a seemingly charmed existence, the mob carried its window-smashing spree along St. James Street and then Piccadilly, passing directly in front of the Home Secretary's home where windows coincidentally escaped damage. At Arlington Street and Piccadilly the mob suddenly came into full view of a squad of twenty policemen, who happened to be there by sheer coincidence. They were the twenty constables from the Vine Street Station. Earlier in the afternoon, Pearson at Scotland Yard, hearing a rumor from the square of a workers' delegation going to Lord Salisbury's Arlington Street residence to give an ovation, dispatched orders for the twenty men of Division C posted at the Vine Street Station under Inspector Knight to move to a position in Arlington Street closer to Salisbury's house. Knight, however, had not been told the reason for his assignment and assumed Lord Salisbury's residence was thought to be in danger of attack. Thus upon seeing the uncontrolled mob in Piccadilly he made no move to intercept it, thinking it inappropriate to desert the post he had been assigned. In this way the mob passed unchallenged in full view of the only remaining police patrol in the West End. Frantic looting began as shop windows were shattered along Piccadilly. The mob broke into Raffini's Tonic Wine Shop, broke brandy bottles and drank the contents from cupped hands. They plundered at least one clothing store, stopped several carriages and demanded money from the occupants.[14]

It was 4:30 when word of the attack on the Carlton reached Dunlop back in the square, who mentioned the information to Walker. Walker had not even known of the one hundred reserves thought to have been sent to Pall Mall and, together with Dunlop, he walked down to Pall Mall to see for himself. He then took the time to send Dunlop up to see the club secretary to procure the number of windows broken and the names of the theft victims. Also unaware of the existence of a telephone at the War Office next door, Walker himself ran back to Scotland Yard with his new information.

Baffled by the unexpected sighting of a mob in Piccadilly, Inspector Knight, while remaining in Arlington Street, sent a sergeant back to the Vine Street Station with this information. The officer on duty there telegraphed the report to Marylebone Station and Marlborough Mews, but not to Scotland Yard. Several off-duty constables scrambled into their coats and dashed out to Piccadilly, but by that time the mob had disappeared down Piccadilly. Meanwhile Knight had left his men to guard Salisbury's house and had run to locate a superior. He found Hume, still guarding Buckingham Palace, who instructed him to go back to his force.

At Hyde Park Corner the crowd split into two groups, one following Burns and the other socialist leaders into the park, and the other maintaining a course through the streets of the West End. The latter group, estimated at between four hundred and one thousand, committed the most serious window-smashing and looting of the afternoon along Audley Street and Oxford Street between 4:30 and five o'clock. Audley Street South was perhaps the most fashionable and prestigious street in the West End, having housed such figures as Boswell, Lord Bute, Charles X, Louis XVIII, and, in 1820, Queen Caroline. Here the mob met only one other constable along its route, at South Audley Street and Mount Street. A very young and inexperienced constable, he remained at his post, but discreetly made no move to interfere.

Information about the still unchallenged rioters in South Audley Street finally reached police in Marylebone Station through a passerby. Inspector Cuthbert and fifteen constables rushed from the station, located the rioters and charged. One of the constables received a severe head cut, but the mob, which had for so long eluded police and committed so much havoc, was easily dispersed when directly challenged. Cuthbert was later strongly commended for his vigorous action.[15] The fifteen constables were also able to take three of the rioters into custody; two painters and a laborer, all from East London.

Once in Hyde Park Burns climbed on the Achilles statue to give yet another speech while many in the crowd were struggling into their new but ill-fitting shirts. He regretted the property damage, alleging that enemies of the socialists had tried to disgrace their movement; Hyndman and Williams spoke in a similar vein. By this time the meeting had attracted the notice of the regular Hyde Park police, twelve on foot and five mounted, under the command of Inspector Bradley. Unaware as yet of the damage just perpetrated, and the meeting being orderly, the Park police merely observed the crowd, which soon dispersed without further incident.

Lack of adequate communications and a sequence of misapprehensions had placed the police in an extremely embarrassing light. Hume had remained idly posted outside Buckingham Palace the whole afternoon and was to learn of the rioting only through passersby. Knight and his men were still outside Salisbury's house at 7:30 that evening, no action having taken place there whatever. Of the three hundred twenty reserves in Scotland Yard, one hundred fifty never left the premises. Scotland Yard did not learn of the riot until well after the long escapade had run its course. Walker remained in Trafalgar Square until near seven o'clock directing traffic totally unaware even at that hour of what had taken place in the West End. The impression of egregious police bungling was inescapable. Burns himself later expressed the belief that had it not been for the "stupid blunder" by which police were sent to The Mall instead of Pall Mall, the whole affair might never have occurred.[16] Harcourt wrote to Chamberlain, "The riot of yesterday was a nasty business, the police seem to have been culpably off their guard."[17]

As far as Childers was concerned, Hamilton's diary perhaps most fairly assessed the situation: "It is an ugly business for the new Home Secretary, who, though of course not really to blame, has to bear the brunt. Sir E. Henderson was evidently caught napping....Poor Childers! I am very sorry for him. He is certainly the most unlucky of men."[18]

The sudden outbreak of such a serious disturbance in the heart of the West End sent a shudder of fear throughout the Metropolis. Was it so unreasonable to assume that what had taken place in Paris during the Commune only fifteen years before might be repeated in England? The more radical of the socialists were referring more and more to the French experience. In Trafalgar Square itself on the Monday of the riot Burns and the others had ranted about French lampposts decorated with the heads of capitalists. The unemployed provided just the right material for socialist revolutionary doctrine and Monday had shown what could happen at almost any time.

On Tuesday many shopkeepers shuttered or barricaded their shops. Police patrols in the West End were reinforced and two omnibuses were hired and brought to Scotland Yard for emergency transport of reserves. The Home Office directed the War Office to have stand-by troops at Chelsea, Wellington and Knightsbridge Barracks and also sent magistrates to each on Tuesday evening to act as legal officers in case of need.[19]

Although Tuesday passed off with no reappearance of the danger, on Wednesday an unusually dense fog descended over the city which perhaps rendered more ominous the electrifying rumor that a mob of seventy five thousand unemployed from Deptford and Greenwich were marching on the West End, wrecking and pillaging along the way. In view of what had transpired on Monday, the news did not seem all that implausible and placards appeared all over the West End, "London in Danger from Socialist Plots." Telegrams of warning poured into Scotland Yard, and the police compounded the panic by forwarding these unsubstantiated reports to West End shopkeepers. Most shops were shuttered by noon and factory owners frantically barricaded their gates. One firm's engineers made preparations to defend the premises by means of fire hoses attached to cauldrons of boiling water. The Bank of England maintained a special guard throughout the day. The Houses of Parliament shut down and the huge iron gates at Charing Cross were closed.[20]

A meeting of the unemployed at Cumberland Market that evening drew sizable numbers of the criminal classes attracted by the opportunities presented by the fog and a large concentration of people. A few broken windows were reported.

But the uglier rumors proved entirely unsubstantial. No Jack Cade appeared and by Thursday the shops reopened and London returned to normal. Hamilton correctly characterized the exaggerated precautions in terms of "the proverbial stable door closed when it is too late." The riot itself was a mere accident, concluded Hamilton, "and though a very unfortunate one, John Bull is not likely to become a French communist."[21]

Although there is no doubt that the SDF gained increased notoriety from its participation in the incident, other socialists disapproved of the whole affair, notably William Morris and the Socialist League.[22] Frederick Engels wrote to Bebel that the mob comprised only "stray rabble rather than unemployed workmen, and had brought further discredit upon socialists."[23]

Damages reached staggering figures, perhaps as high as £ 50,000, mostly from broken windows. Merchants filed 281 claims for riot compensation.[24] The merchants of Bond Street and portions of Oxford Street whose shops were saved by the police interception presented to Cuthbert a gold watch, £ 2.2 to his inspector, 25 shillings each to his three sergeants and a guinea to each of the constables.[25]

The only tangible gain registered by the demonstrations was a suspiciously sudden doubling of the Mansion House Fund for poor relief in the City. Hyndman claimed the Fund rose from £ 3,000 to £ 75,000 in the forty-eight hours following the riot. During the week the four socialist colleagues, Burns, Hyndman, Williams, and Champion, tried to gain an audience with Chamberlain at the Local Government Board but without success. In response to a written deposition he promised nothing more than a guarded assurance of possibly increased outdoor relief. But the dispensation of charity was still a totally local affair and while the City might be able to afford vastly increased largesse, most

districts of East London could not. The notion of national assistance was far in the future. Gladstone, one week after the Pall Mall
Affair, wrote that "the bulk of the working classes are (comparatively) not ill but well off, through the cheapness of commodities,
especially provisions: to make the State minister to the poor of
London at the expense of the nation would be dangerous in principle."[26]

For the new Home Secretary, the whole affair was acutely embarrassing, a cruel introduction to the new post. He confided his
frustrations in a letter to his son just four days later:

> I took over this department between eleven and twelve, and the
> heads of the police told me that all necessary preparations had been
> made, and, of course, I could not have made any change even had I
> wished. But all the trouble of inquiry falls on me, and the Police are
> greatly discredited, part of this discredit being reflected on the Home
> Office.[27]

In a letter from Paris his daughter Emily wrote for more money
and commiserated about "...these horrible riots. What a shame of
them to begin, just the day you took office, or rather began work.
London must be horrible just now."[28]

The greatest embarrassment accrued from the hour and a half
time lag between the first stoning at the Carlton and the actual
police intervention in Audley Street. Childers himself learned of
the rioting long before notification by the police. His wife sent
a note to him from their home in Piccadilly just after the mob
passed their house, informing him of the death of an uncle and
also of the narrow escape. Up to that point, no one at the Home
Office had had any intimation of the disturbance.

The Parliamentary Committee of Inquiry which Childers
formed (and chaired) heard testimony for four days and placed
the blame squarely on the Metropolitan police. Childers reluctantly
felt compelled to accept the resignation of his old friend as Chief
Commissioner. Henderson had directed the force for seventeen
years, appointed initially in 1869 by Bruce, who had remained a
close friend ever since and who now gave Henderson's eulogy in
the House of Lords.[29] Henderson's only-partially stoical attitude
is reflected in his answer to a letter of sympathy from Harcourt,
another good friend with whom he had worked for over five
years:

> That my flank should have been turned by my standing enemies
> the roughs, after seventeen years of successful warfare on our side, is

"Mob in St. James Street, Opposite the New University Club"

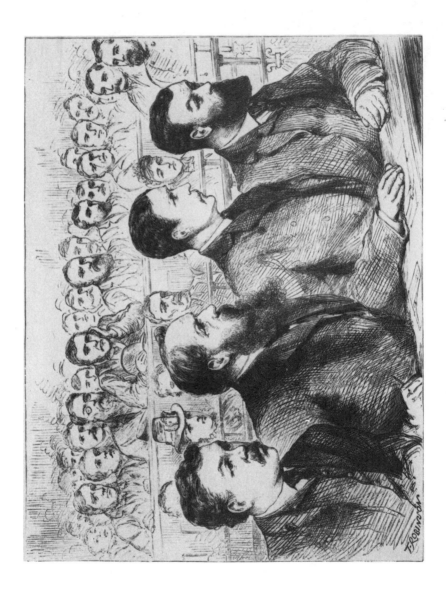

"Examination of the Social Democratic Federation Leaders at Bow-Street Police Court"

Sir Edmund Henderson

Sir Charles Warren

a matter of great regret. One thing, I do not think after this experience, it need ever be feared again, but of course the future of the great force I have so long commanded, rests no more with me.[30]

The Queen wondered why the Home Secretary could not forbid such disgraceful scenes in the capital.[31] She was also miffed at not being informed promptly enough of Henderson's accepted resignation and Gladstone tried to excuse it as an unintentional oversight on the part of the new Home Secretary.[32]

The press demanded government prosecution of the SDF ring-leaders, a sentiment echoed by merchants, the Fair Traders, and most non-socialist citizens of the West End. Following consultations with Harcourt and his own legal advisors, Childers ordered the arrest of the four socialists. They were served summonses on Saturday the 13th, charged with seditious conspiracy on the 17th and released on bail, William Morris standing bail for Burns and Champion. Burns was later to lionize himself in his recollections of every stage of the proceedings. His superior attitude is most humorously shown in his own narration of the manner of his initial arrest on the 13th:

> ...I saw a hansom cab coming in our direction. Now a hansom cab in Nine Elms Road in those days was something of an event. People came out to look at it. Something must be doing. I thought I recognised [sic] the man in it. I held up my hand to the driver to stop him. He knew me, as most of the cabmen did, and pulled up.
>
> 'Well, what is it?' said the man in the hansom, rather testily.
>
> 'Excuse me,' I said, 'but I think you are on your way out to Battersea.'
>
> 'Well, what of it?' he said. He did not recognise me.
>
> 'And in the pocket of your coat there you have a summons which you intend to serve on John Burns?'
>
> He flushed up, for he recognized me then. He got out of the cab, and we walked along together towards Vauxhall. He made himself most agreeable. What hat [sic] do you think we discussed as we walked along? The pictures of Gimabue [sic] and Giotto. Then when we got to Vauxhall he said: 'Look here! Where can I serve this summons on you?'
>
> I took him into the Station, and there, behind the door, before the Booking Office, he took out the blue paper from his pocket, and read it over to me.[33]

Burns always managed to assume a commanding role, even while being arrested, at least in his own mind.

While the four socialists were awaiting trial, they proclaimed their defiance by calling for another socialist demonstration for the unemployed in Hyde Park on the 21st. Determined not to be embarrassed a second time, Childers ordered not only extra police, but troops to be placed in readiness at Chelsea, Knightsbridge, Wellington, St. George's and Regent's Park Barracks. Henderson, who was remaining at his post pending the arrival from India of his successor (Sir Charles Warren), this time took the added precaution of issuing pencils and slips of paper to each superintendent, inspector and sergeant and ordering all messages to be delivered in writing. Telegrams were to be sent back to Scotland Yard every quarter hour.[34] The socialists, too, wishing to provide concrete proof of the nonviolent, responsible actions of their four charged leaders, themselves appealed for extra police attendance and in the event, conducted a very orderly series of meetings. Burns, still brandishing his now-famous red flag, commenced his own speech by asking that the day's demonstration be peaceful and orderly in view of the legally perilous position of himself and the others. But he terminated defiantly with a rousing call for social revolution:

> Why did hungry men commit violence? Was it because they were inherently vicious? No, but because they saw before them idlers enjoying the wealth they had produced.
> He had spoken prophetically a fortnight ago in Trafalgar Square; he was going to do so then. If the Government did not comply with their demands, worse than what they had seen throughout the world must of necessity happen.

Prosecution, imprisonment, even death held no fears for Burns: "They had put their hands to the plough; they did not intend to go back until the people's cause was won..."[35]

As the estimated fifty thousand demonstrators began to disperse a small scuffle ensued with perhaps overly-nervous police, but on the whole the giant meeting passed off peacefully.[36]

The rare sedition trial began in Old Bailey courtroom on April 6 and lasted five days. The State had charged the four individually with nine counts of sedition and as a group with one count of seditious conspiracy. The Government prosecution was led by the Attorney General, Sir Charles Russell, whose behavior throughout strongly suggested some doubts as to the course he had been directed to take. He presented what would seem in this day to have been a very weak and half-hearted case, deferring too accommodatingly to every objection of the defendants. The State made no objection to the unusually wide latitude the court gave the defendants. The prosecution called only four witnesses, three of whom were quite neutral reporters, and the fourth a cricket batmaker for the police.

The prosecution specifically exonerated the defendants of any intention to incite to acts of violence, but "the prosecution was glad to say" there was ample evidence that they throughout took action to prevent damage and pillage. The Attorney General gratuitously volunteered further that the evidence indicated the defendants "did not intend disturbances to take place." The sole charges consisted of a few phrases alleged to have been used during the speeches such as "unless we get bread, they must have lead," and "We have shown them today what we can do with stones; and unless they do something for us we will show them what we can do with powder and shot."

Champion and Hyndman conducted their own defense. Mr. Thompson, representing Williams and Burns, pointed out that in England a fairly "rough and ready" manner of speaking was commonly tolerated in public meetings, especially outdoors. The basis of the defense was that the language of the defendants, though admittedly intemperate, had not seriously exceeded these norms. Examples of similarly strong language was adduced from the speeches of Chamberlain, of Randolph Churchill, of Gladstone himself. Actually the remark Burns made about the heads decorating lampposts in France was originally made by Chamberlain (in reference to Foulon).

The defense called witness after witness to testify either that they had not heard the seditious language or that they identified it as coming from someone other than the defendants. Stead briefly testified for the defendants, facing Sir Charles Russell, who had only three months earlier helped conduct Stead's unsuccessful defense in his morals charge.

Burns was allowed to deliver a lengthy and aggressive speech in his own defense. He denied the phrases "bread or lead" and "powder and shot" but made no apologies for other statements. He blamed all the damage on the Carlton Club hecklers and lack of police protection along the route. Burns then launched into what can only be characterized as a socialist polemic. Society, not the Social Democrats, was to blame for any rioting that had taken place. The Attorney General ought to have prepared indictments against Society. He had no regrets for his part in the agitation. The riot was "nothing more nor less than honest poverty knocking at the door of selfish luxury and comfort...." It was the social system which prompts men to thievery and women to prostitution by not assuring to all a fair start in life. As for seditious conspiracy, "the 650 members of the House are as guilty as we are." The State's prosecution was a panic prosecution, based on the most inconclusive evidence. Prison had no terror for him—it was better to die in prison than to die starving. Burns concluded his polemic by calling for the jury by their verdict to stigmatize the State prosecution as "absurd, stupid and frivolous."[37]

Many years later, after John Burns completed his political conversion to the Establishment and had entered not only Parliament but the Local Government Board, Hyndman would charge that the speech was not Burns', but that he, Hyndman, and Champion had written it for him.[38] For his part Burns later remarked that Hyndman "acted like a craven" in the dock.[39]

The judge himself dismissed the tenth count of conspiracy and the jury deliberated only an hour and fifteen minutes before returning a verdict of acquittal for all four defendants on the remaining charges. The right of public meeting never became an issue although the defendants tried to inject it into the case.

Two years later, on the anniversary of his acquittal, Burns wrote in his diary "I think it would have done [the movement] more good if we had all got twelve months, but we were not so fortunate."[40] The trial became increasingly glamorized in his recollection as the years passed. By 1893 he had been on trial for his life and had expected ten years.[41] Though Burns escaped in 1886, events of the next year were to lead him to a more serious trial and real imprisonment.

1. William Kent, *John Burns, Labour's Lost Leader*, p. 24.

2. Joseph Burgess, *John Burns*, p. 48. Burgess was a free-lance newsman at the time and the Pall Mall Affair created a boom for him. "I made good money out of those disturbances, which set me on my feet with the Fleet

Street sub-editors as a man with a good nose for exclusive Labour and Socialist news." (p. 42).

3. H.H. Asquith, *Fifty Years of Parliament*, Vol. I, p. 136.

4. For the most detailed account, see Great Britain, *Parliamentary Papers*, Vol. XXXIV (1886), C. 4665, "Report of a Committee to inquire and report as to the Origin and Character of the Disturbances which took Place in the Metropolis on Monday, the 8th of February, and as to the Conduct of the Police authorities in Relation thereto; with Minutes of Evidence and Appendix." Hereafter referred to as "Evidence."

5. Burgess, p. 52.

6. "Evidence," Q. 1375.

7. Burgess, p. 54.

8. Ibid., pp. 55, 56.

9. Burns Papers, B.M. Add. Mss., 46308 f. 40.

10. "Evidence," Q. 554.

11. "Evidence," Q. 631, 938, 1083, 1501.

12. Burns Papers, 46308 f. 40, 41. See also G.D.H. Cole, *British Working Class Politics 1832-1914*, p. 95.

13. "Evidence," Q. 408.

14. Burgess, 65 ff. G.D.H. Cole, *John Burns*, 10-13. John Mackail, *Life of William Morris*, Vol. II, p. 151. Cole exonerates the SDF from any blame in association with the looting. Burgess claimed "the leaders of the S.D.F. were genuinely afraid of the Frankenstein that had been raised." (p. 63).

15. P.R.O. MEPOL 2/182.

16. Burns Papers, 46308 f. 40. Burgess too claimed the violence was unpremeditated. "Had there been any decent force of police on duty, the mob would never have gat [sic] out of hand." (p. 45).

17. Harcourt Papers, correspondence, Harcourt to Chamberlain, February 9, 1886. See also *Pall Mall Gazette*, February 9, 1886.

18. Hamilton Papers, B.M. Add. Mss., 48643, Diary for February 9, 1886.

19. P.R.O. MEPOL 2/182.

20. *Annual Register* (1886) I, 46 and II, 7; Henry Hyndman, *Record of an Adventurous Life*, p. 370; Dona Torr, *Tom Mann and His Times*, I, 227; Peter Clayden, *England Under the Coalition*, pp. 20, 21.

21. Hamilton Papers, Diary for February 9, 1886.

22. Cole, p. 155.

23. Torr, p. 228.

24. *Annual Register* (1886) II, 9.

25. P.R.O. MEPOL 2/182.

26. Gladstone Papers, B.M. Add. Mss. 44548 f. 105, 106. Gladstone to Ponsonby, February 16, 1886.

27. E.S.E. Childers, *The Life and Correspondence of the Rt. Hon. Hugh Culling Eardley Childers*, Vol. II, p. 240.

28. Childers Papers, Royal Commonwealth Society 22/105.

29. *3 Hansard* (Lords) CCCII (1886), 1012-1017, February 23.

30. Harcourt Papers, Henderson to Harcourt, February 24, 1886.

31. George E. Buckle, ed., *The Letters of Queen Victoria*, Vol. I, pp. 52-54.

32. Gladstone to Ponsonby, February 24, 1886. Gladstone Papers, B.M. Add. Mss. 44548 f. 112.

33. Burns Papers, 46308 f. 38-39.
34. HO 45/B158/4.
35. Burgess, pp. 76-79.
36. *Annual Register* (1886) II, 8, 9.
37. John Burns, *The Man With the Red Flag. Being the Speech Delivered at the Old Bailey* (1886).
38. Burgess, viii.
39. Burgess, 189; London *Star*, January 23, 1894.
40. Burns Papers, Diary for April 10, 1888, B.M. Add. Mss. 46310 f. 26.
41. Kent, p. 53.

9

THE STRUGGLE FOR TRAFALGAR SQUARE

Eighteen eighty-seven was jubilee year. "There never was anything like the excitement about the Jubilee. One hears nothing but 'Jubilee, Jubilee, Jubilee,' morning noon and night." Jubilee Day was June 21 and the weather was fine. The crowds were enthusiastic and good-humored. Hamilton noted in his diary:

> The most remarkable feature of the evening was the extraordinary good nature and orderliness of the crowds in the streets. A few years ago festivity and drunkenness were among the masses almost synonymous terms....We can flatter ourselves that we have recently become far more orderly and sober and have made great advances in the art of organization. Rowdyism and rough horseplay which have usually characterized large English assemblies have become conspicuous by their absence.[1]

It is most extraordinary that less than six months after this was written Trafalgar Square was the scene of a mélee so rough and sanguinary it has come to be called "Bloody Sunday."

A riotous massacre in Trafalgar Square followed by a general strike, the collapse of the Government—these are the preludes to William Morris' utopian socialist millenium in *News from Nowhere*. By the time the development of the Square had been completed, it had indeed become one of the focal points of mass demonstration, as well as one of London's most popular public squares. Most of the work on the Square itself, including the two fountains and Nelson's Column, was complete by mid-century. The bronze capitol of the column was cast from the cannon recovered from the wreck of the Royal George. The four bronze lions appeared in 1867. In 1875 the official standards of measurement were etched in lengths of bronze along the north wall. Fashionably bordered on the north by the National Gallery, on the east by St. Martins-in-the-fields and Morley's Hotel, on the south by Whitehall, and on the west by the Union Club and the College of Physicians, the Square became a sort of national symbol by the 1880s.

The addition of wooden benches donated by Lord Brabazon made the Square especially attractive to London vagrants. Increasingly they took over the Square at night, if not with police authorization, then at least with their acquiescence. Police reported little or no trouble from them, and as vagrancy laws were customarily interpreted in terms of charity rather than punishment, there appeared at first little reason to interfere. In August 1887, an eighteen-year-old girl charged with fighting in Convent Garden was asked in Bow Street Court where she lived. "Nowhere." "Where do you sleep?" "Trafalgar Square." The answer seemed to surprise no one. Chief Superintendent Dunlop (of division A which included Trafalgar Square) explained during the summer of 1887 that "the police do not interfere with these poor houseless creatures, in fact it would be sad, I think to do so, after wandering all day without food. It would require a sterner heart than I possess to refuse them a temporary escape from their troubles in sleep."[2] Although the neighborhood Casual Wards routinely provided free accommodation and reported that it hardly ever had to turn anyone away for lack of space, it appears that many of the Square regulars simply preferred the Square to the Casual Wards. Gradually more fashionable Londoners came to include Trafalgar Square on their nightly slumming excursions. John Burns escorted three ladies to the Square one August night and explained to a constable they had come "to see the tramps." For the ladies it was quite predictably, "a horrid sight." In the predawn hours passersby enjoyed tossing coppers down into the Square and watching the scramble. Customarily the tramps melted away with daylight, and the Square returned to normal. It was much the same at many other London parks and open spaces.

It was during the summer of 1887 that various charitable organizations "discovered" the Trafalgar Square vagrants and proceeded to donate meal and lodging tickets. The Reverend Thomas Jackson staged meetings at 3:30 in the morning followed by the distribution of breakfast tickets at 5:00 A.M. These and other attentions evoked a change in the life-style of the Square regulars,

more and more of whom tended to remain in the Square throughout much of the day. The obvious bounties drew larger numbers
and they became far more visible than ever before. They washed
themselves and their clothes in the fountain; they lounged on the
benches and the monument.[3]

The socialists and radicals were especially quick to sense the
new opportunities in Trafalgar Square for the propagation of their
causes. Some were no doubt well-meaning, others exploitative, but
each group saw clearly the advantages in becoming spokesman for
the clustered unemployed, who in turn welcomed the attentions
as a diversion from the otherwise grim monotony of their lives.
They were a captive audience in a truly pathetic sense and willing
participants in virtually any foray the agitators might dream up.

John Burns was at the time working as the sole electrical engineer in a small factory in Westminster owned by a member of
the Democratic Club, Mr. Lorraine. Following the increased notoriety stemming from his participation in the Pall Mall Affair
he had been blacklisted from most of the larger factories. The
sympathetic attitude of his new employer made it possible for
Burns to obtain time off to attend many of these meetings and he
was a frequent speaker. The socialists also organized "Church
Parades" which converged on London churches during Sunday
services. It was Burns who led one of the largest such processions
to St. Paul's in early 1887. Banners read "My house is a house of
prayer, but you have made it a den of thieves."[4] The more out-
rageous the spectacle, reasoned the organizers, the greater the
advertisement for their cause.

In early October the socialists appeared in Trafalgar Square with
a fife and drum band. An almost daily series of programs was in-
augurated. On the 14th they led a procession of 2,000 unemployed, marching behind a black flag, to the Mansion House. The
Lord Mayor refused to see them. They staged a Square rally to
protest the sentencing of the Chicago anarchists. The chairman at
this meeting was the Reverend Stewart Headlam, a prominent
Christian Socialist minister, and speakers included not only Burns
but several noted socialist leaders: William Morris, George Bernard
Shaw, Annie Besant, the American Henry George, whose *Progress
and Poverty* had become one of the most influential books in

England in the eighties, and the Russian anarchists Kropotkin and
Stepniak.[5] During the next month the socialists sponsored almost
daily demonstrations of the unemployed.

On a typical day the unemployed began to congregate at
Nelson's Column around noon, and meetings got under way by
1:00 p.m. After several hours of speeches, the demonstrators
passed appropriate resolutions and then marched off to various
parts of London. During mid-October these processions became increasingly disorderly, and minor disturbances took place at Westminister Abbey, the Mansion House, and in Hyde Park. On the
19th a serious collision occurred between the police and the
processionists in Piccadilly.[6]

While the organizers saw the unemployed congregations as
prospective new converts to their cause, ordinary citizens saw only
tramps and vagrants. Residents of the area were scandalized by
the unsavory appearance of the Square and its new occupants.
Tradesmen suffered loss of business; traffic was disrupted; the
noise, the smells, the language, and the disorders outraged the
the more affluent. The unemployed had clearly become a real
nuisance.

A trickle of complaints from irate residents soon increased to
a torrent. Neighborhood tradesmen perhaps justifiably attributed
a sharp decline in business to daily scenes of disorder in the
Square. Banks, jewelers and hotels complained of dwindling
security. The banking firm of Ranson Bouverie and Co. at the
corner of Pall Mall East had installed iron shutters following the
Pall Mall riot of the year before. During the Trafalgar Square
demonstrations throughout October and early November the
bank's clerks and attendants stood guard with truncheons and a
smaller amount of cash was kept on the premises.[7] Everyone felt
the inconvenience of traffic congestion. Protests and petitions
flooded the offices of authority. The Royal College of Physicians
complained of "insufferable" annoyance caused by the daily noise
and tumult. Extra police were assigned to patrol near banks and
jewelers, but there was no appreciable improvement of business.
A member of the National Liberal Club reported at Bow Street
Police Court that during the meeting on October 23 he heard an
orator threaten that the unemployed would purposely ruin the
local trade by incessant processions so as to force the business

community to recognize and meet their demands.[8] Delegations of businessmen and professional men deluged the Home Office with protests and petitions for relief from the "terrorism" which had allegedly become commonplace in the area.

At the Home Office after the Conservative "victory" at the polls in 1886 was Henry Matthews, the first Roman Catholic to achieve cabinet rank since the passage of the Emancipation Act. Born in Ceylon, he was descended from the Welsh family of Matthew of Llandaff. Educated at the Universities of Paris and London, he earned highest honors in Classics and Mathematics, the two traditionally most fashionable disciplines in Victorian schools. He was admitted to the bar after Lincoln's Inn. Independently wealthy and unmarried, he spent a good deal of his time hunting or socializing, dining regularly at the Anthenaeum or Carlton Club. In 1868 he won election in the Welsh constituency of Dungarvan admittedly "...at the cost of 800 bottles of whiskey,"[9] but lost in 1874 and again in 1880. He was an able barrister involved in many difficult cases, including that of Dilke, in which he conducted the cross-examination. His close friend, Lord Randolph Churchill, urged him to stand for North Birmingham in 1885 where he lost again, but Matthews won East Birmingham the following year and Lord Randolph persuaded Salisbury to offer his friend the Home Office. "Going from law to politics is like going from the company of the most virtuous and highminded (tho' somewhat dull) ladies into that of ladies of a very dubious character,"[10] was Matthews' description of his own transition.

Whatever premonitions Matthews harbored about political life were quickly substantiated. Buffeted in the House over police handling of a case of solicitation in July 1887, the extremely critical Hamilton concluded, "He has certainly not been a success as Home Secretary. There are rumors that he meditates retirement."[11] Hamilton was a difficult man to please. Matthews' greatest challenge, however, came from the Trafalgar Square demonstrators.

From the very first meeting of early October 1887, Police Commissioner Sir Charles Warren had maintained a close surveillance of the socialist-unemployed demonstrations and processions. He personally attended many of the meetings to assess for himself the character of the crowds and considered them potentially very

Henry Matthews

dangerous. He ordered that all processions departing from the Square were to be followed by police wherever they went. But as the numbers increased, so did public pressure to ban the meetings altogether. Matthews was fully sympathetic with Warren's dilemma. The extreme difficulty of dealing legally with such wandering groups was virtually unprecedented. They constituted for the most part merely a nuisance but were nevertheless always a a source of potential danger, composed as they were of a large percentage of youthful roughs. Their assemblies were not illegal and their processions fell short of what might properly be termed disturbances. But due to the danger inherent in their composition, they had always to be attended or followed closely by police.

The demonstrations were straining the resources of the Metropolitan Police, and this may have had some bearing on Warren's indecision. Matthews had already augmented the force slightly during the summer. In a letter to Salisbury in late October he referred to the excessive demands on the police created by the "carnival of roughs."[12] On Monday, October 17, Warren decided to take action. He proclaimed a temporary but unconditional ban on all meetings in Trafalgar Square. He later justified his decision on pragmatic grounds:

> That proclamation was in my judgment absolutely necessary in the interests of public peace. I do not consider that the danger to the public peace depends on what appears on the face of the placard calling the meeting. I took care to give directions that the mobs amd bands of people should be surrounded so that they could not loot. I thought that was absolutely necessary. In my opinion it is not safe to wait till a breach of the peace has actually taken place before taking police measures.[13]

For three days police enforced the ban against only token resistance. But Matthews urged Warren to suspend the ban on October 19, pending a legal opinion. Thus the meetings and processions were again permitted for the remainder of the month. Troops were requisitioned and stood by in case of need. But the result of such ostensible capriciousness was that the organizers were encouraged rather than deterred.

In late October the Home Office requested a Law Office Opinion on the legality of a proposed one-month ban on processions under the provisions of the Metropolitan Police Act (2 & 3 Vict. c 47,

Sect 52-54). Warren, anxiously awaiting the reply, wrote to
Matthews on October 31:

> The position becomes every day more and more difficult to deal
> with, and the mob, which at first was disorganized is now beginning to
> obtain a certain amount of cohesion; from constant practice the roughs
> are beginning to find exactly what they can do with impunity....It
> is now apparent that the policy of the mob leaders is to settle in private
> their tactics for each day how to elude the Police and I think it more
> than probable that they will get out of hand in a very short time if
> they are not dispersed.
>   ...The reports I receive on all sides make me feel that the condition
> of the mob is getting very disquieting; by some private signal they
> appear to be able to get together now to the number of 2 or 3,000 in
> two or three minutes....[14]

Hopes for a legal prohibition were dashed on November 1 by
the L.O.O. signed by Webster and Clarke to the effect that the
statute did not justify such a blanket prohibition as was proposed.
At the same time, Lord Mayor's Day (November 9) was approaching
and the language of the orators became more and more flagrantly
inflammatory. On November 1 Alfred Allman, a socialist, urged
the mob to "terrorize the old scoundrel" (the Lord Mayor) and
stage a "big riot" on his day. Next day an un-named speaker was
reported as shouting: "stand shoulder to shoulder and fight the
police, and upset everything that stands against us...strike a blow
like Englishmen."[15] On November 3 Warren, who had attended
the afternoon's meeting, issued general instructions to police to
arrest any person who used threatening language, with Matthews'
approval. By this time Lord Randolph had become very much
dissappointed in his nominee, "...in whom he expected to find
some willingness to go ahead; instead of which Matthews was
Tory of Tories."[16] The Tory radical had himself resigned in pique
the preceding year.

An unusually large crowd of 1,500 gathered in Trafalgar Square
on Friday, November 4, and Superintendent Sheppard personally
acquainted the speakers with the new regulations at the commence-
ment of the meeting. In spite of this warning, the regular daily
chairman, a man called Lynch, declared that "the police were very
much mistaken if they thought they could stop twenty to thirty
thousand of the unemployed gathering on the ninth and bringing
a dozen granite stones in their pockets to throw at the Lord Mayor's
carriage." Allman, another regular speaker, then announced de-

fiantly that he intended to preach "sedition," and at this point police arrested both men and the crowd dispersed. On Sunday the 6th, police allowed a morning meeting but prohibited an afternoon one. Headlam remarked that if Jesus Christ came to Trafalgar Square, He would find Himself under arrest in short order.[17]

As Lord Mayor's Day approached, Warren obtained Home Office permission to take further precautions. On Monday, November 7, he issued an order banning all processions on Wednesday except, of course, the Lord Mayor's. A crowd of nine hundred assembled in Trafalgar Square on Tuesday, raised a red flag and tried to organize a procession, which the police blocked. Then Comrade George, another popular speaker, suggested demonstrating on Lord Mayor's Day in defiance of Warren's ban, and police promptly arrested him and two journalists, the latter on charges of obstructing the police.[18]

On the eve of Lord Mayor's Day, Charles Warren threw down the final gauntlet. With the approval of the Home Office and the Board of Works he ordered a general ban on all further Trafalgar Square meetings or demonstrations on grounds that the area was Crown property. Orders for four thousand placards were placed that same evening to be delivered by 2:30 A.M. the following morning. Messrs. Willing & Co. handled the public posting which was accomplished by 8:00 A.M. The placard read:

> In consequence of the disorderly scenes which have recently occurred in Trafalgar Square...and with a view to preventing such disorderly proceedings and to preserve the public peace, I Charles Warren, the Commissioner of the Police of the Metropolis, do hereby give notice, with the sanction of the Secretary of State, and concurrence of the Commissioners of Her Majesty's Works and Public Buildings that... until further intimation, no public meetings will be allowed to assemble in Trafalgar Square, nor will speeches be allowed to be delivered therein.[19]

This ban was not to be lifted for nearly five years, until October, 1892.

The outcry against "repression of free speech" was predictably not long in coming, although inclement weather resolved all of Warren's apprehensions for Lord Mayor's Day. A steady downpour accompanied the procession, as well as an imposing display of police, and the socialists abandoned all threats to stage any sort of counter-demonstration. Continued wet weather facilitated the enforcement of Warren's ban for the remainder of the week. But the organizers were merely delayed by the rain, and by Friday plans were well underway for a Sunday mass demonstration. At about this time the agitators discovered another allied cause in the Irish question.

Always smoldering, Irish flames of discount had blazed again in 1887 when Commons, by the Crimes Act, had made it illegal for Irish tenants to resist eviction, even for nonpayment of exorbitant rents. In Catholic Ireland the law was universally despised, widely flouted, and decried by men of high position. One such was William O'Brien, editor of "United Ireland", an arch-Parnellite, and a leading Nationalist in Commons. In August 1887, the authorities prosecuted O'Brien for inciting resistance to the Crimes Act, and summoned him to petty sessions at Michelstown on September 9. He failed to appear, but sympathetic crowds demonstrated in his favor and during the rally police came to blows with people on the periphery of the gathering, and eventually opened fire upon the crowd, killing one person and wounding several others. The incident outraged the Irish, many Liberals and the radicals everywhere, including many in London who, however illogically, tried to associate the violence of Michelstown with Warren's "repression of free speech" in Trafalgar Square. Later in September the courts tried and sentenced O'Brien to prison, where his quixotic refusal to change into prison clothing led to the well-publicized confiscation of his breeches by the warden. "O'Brien's breeches" became for a time the rallying cry of Irish Nationalists, shortly to be taken up also by many socialist and radical groups. Warren's ban on Trafalgar Square meetings provided a unique opportunity to merge the free speech movement with Irish Nationalism in a common attack on the Tory government. On Friday, the 11th of November, the Metropolitan Radical Association announced plans to stage a mammoth demonstration the following Sunday in the forbidden square. Its dual purpose was to protest O'Brien's imprisonment and assert the right of public meeting in Trafalgar Square. The plight of the unemployed was all but forgotten for the time being.

The proposal of the Metropolitan Radical Association received instant support from many Opposition groups in London. The Social Democratic Federation, the Socialist League, the Home Rule Union, anarchist clubs, and all radical clubs immediately entered the contest. Leaders worked frantically on Friday and Saturday to coordinate the efforts of all the various groups. They quickly printed large green posters advertising the demonstration, one titled "Coercion in London—a Radical Meeting Proclaimed." Another read, "The right of public meeting is denied by the ukase of a military and despotic filibuster. Are you prepared to submit? If not, come in tens of thousands. Preserve your dear-bought liberties at all risks."[20]

A last-minute effort to avoid a confrontation was made on Saturday, November 12. The radicals sent a deputation to the Home Office led by Cunninghame Graham, M.P. Matthews refused to see the deputation except for Graham and refused to intervene to rescind the police ban.[21] He then issued another proclamation that evening forbidding any processions to approach Trafalgar Square on the 13th.[22] On the same evening organizers were distributing a memo directing marchers not to bring weapons, sticks or even umbrellas.[23]

Warren's apprehension of a repetition of the previous year's disorders in Pall Mall led him to take extraordinary precautions to enforce his ban. He assigned five thousand constables to Sunday duty, two thousand in and around Trafalgar Square, the remainder positioned strategically to prevent any large contingents from massing for converging marches toward the Square. A magistrate was to stand by armed with the Riot Act. Troops were requisitioned.

Since large numbers were expected from the south side of the Thames, Warren secured all bridges with strong garrisons. Trafalgar Square itself was one sea of blue. Warren himself was present in the Square from early Sunday morning until three o'clock in the afternoon.

By 10:00 A.M. on November 13, 1,500 constables had cordoned off the open spaces of Trafalgar Square, standing two deep shoulder to shoulder all around the central part of the Square and four deep facing Whitehall. Warren stationed an extra three hundred at Nelson's Column, one hundred cavalry police armed with revolvers in front of the Grand Hotel, two thousand five hundred reserve constables in Charing Cross, one hundred at Hyde Park, and scores of other details in all the main thoroughfares leading to Trafalgar Square. A battalion of Grenadier Guards and a regiment of Life Guards were not far away. John Mackail, the biographer of William Morris, thought the elaborate preparations sufficient "to repel something little short of a popular insurrection."[24]

Radical leaders had planned that each of nearly sixty contingent groups should meet in its own neighborhood in the early afternoon, conduct brief rallies, and begin marching toward the Square so as to converge there at exactly 4:00 P.M. The Clerkenwell branch of the London Patriotic Club, one of the largest of the participating radical associations, met in Clerkenwell at 2:00 P.M., where Morris and Shaw each pled for orderliness and determination. Annie Besant denounced the police ban as so much "waste paper." Delegations of the East Finsbury Radical Club, the Socialist League, and the local branches of the Social Democratic Federation arrived by 3:00 P.M. at Clerkenwell. Many of the demonstrators wore red ribbons tied with black crepe; others carried red flags of all sizes. Banners read: "Put your trust in God and keep your powder dry"; "Disobedience to tyrants is a duty to God." At 3:30 P.M. the combined groups moved off toward their rendezvous with the waiting police. Approaching Bloomsbury Street, still one-half mile from the Square, the procession came up face to face with a strong police line, composed of both mounted and infantry constables. When the marchers refused to disperse the police charged, swinging their batons, and easily routed the group, capturing all the banners and large flags. George Bernard Shaw later recalled his less than heroic role in this part of the affair:

> The contingent with which I marched was scattered by a police charge at the north end of Shaftesbury Avenue. I was not personally molested and walked in the capacity of a private gentlemen to Trafalgar Square and 'moved on' round and round it until the affair was over. All the fighting was done by the other contingent. I had no part in it and the police were quite polite to me.... It was over before I arrived.[25]

As Warren had feared, the organizers were successful in attracting huge numbers of demonstrators from South London, from Deptford, Battersea, Bermondsey, Fulham and other neighborhoods. From these areas converging deputations of Irish Nationalists, radicals and socialists formed a mammoth procession of about eight thousand. Wearing green and red armbands and singing the "Marseillaise" and "Starving for Old England," the mass approached Westminister Bridge. A line of police blocked the bridge, but with arms linked the mass forced their way across; the fierce mélee left twenty-six of their number to be taken to St. Thomas' Hospital. On the other side of the bridge, the demonstrators re-formed but were again confronted with police lines at Parliament Street where a second battle took place beneath the Clock Tower. Police estimated this crowd at three to four thousand and the affray lasted some twenty minutes. A stonemason named George Harrison was arrested for assaulting one policeman with an iron gas-pipe and stabbing another with an oyster knife. After having been dispersed, the crowd resumed its progress toward the Square individually or in small parties.

A mob of some five thousand from various sectors of East London was intercepted by police in the Strand near Waterloo Place. Inspector Livingstone was there assaulted by a man wielding a stone in a handkerchief. Livingstone was taken to hospital and was subsequently off duty for seven weeks. Another constable was knocked down and kicked by the crowd. Others were assaulted with timber and iron bars.[26] At Duncannon Street, nearer the Square, police intercepted a large van which was found to contain a huge quantity of sticks, stones and other suitable missiles.[27]

The success of the police in breaking up the massed processions did not prevent most of the demonstrators from reaching the environs of the Square individually. But they thereby lost all cohesion and effectiveness and were virtually swallowed up by thousands of sightseers and spectators. Prevented from entering the Square itself by Warren's strong police cordon, the crowds of demonstrators and curiosity-seekers milled out in the streets abutting the Square. *The Times* estimated the size of the crowd by mid-afternoon at twenty thousand; the police estimated the numbers at forty to fifty thousand.[28]

By prearrangement, Burns and his friends were to meet at Charing Cross at four o'clock and then force their way to Nelson's Column to hold their meeting. But Burns could not locate any of his friends except Hyndman and Graham. Better known by his friends as Don Roberto, Robert Bontine Cunninghame Graham was the well-to-do son of a Scottish laird, world traveler, author, and since 1886 a Member of Parliament (for N.W. Lanarkshire). Tall and gentlemanly, imposing in top hat, he looked a most un-likely partner for the short, roughened, proletarian Burns. Hyndman was carrying an umbrella, which Graham advised him to leave behind, and the three of them, together with some others, advanced down the Strand toward the Square. As they reached Morley's Hotel just at the corner of the Square, Hyndman somehow became separated from the other two and took no part in the actual assault on the Square.

At the signal "Now for the Square" a group of men variously estimated at from two hundred to four hundred, armed with sticks and stones, made a rush at the police line. Burns and Graham, arms linked, led the frontal attack. The time was almost exactly 4:00 P.M. The demonstrators hit the police cordon at full tilt, fists flailing. Graham smashed a constable full in the face, knocking off his helmet and cutting his lip. He was taken into custody with considerably rough treatment:

> I was seized by the police. Two constables seized me, one by each shoulder. Another pulled me by the ear from behind, and a fourth struck me on the head with his truncheon. Other blows were struck on various parts of my body, and the policeman who cut my head was making a second blow when Burns raised his folded arms above his head and rushed between us to ward off the blow.[29]

Burns was also arrested, but the police could not easily deal with the rougher elements among their attackers who were throwing stones and striking them with sticks. The police then drew their staves, but still were unable immediately to stem the advance. The two hundred Life Guards stationed at Whitehall were then called in, accompanied by a magistrate with the Riot Act. While a police surgeon attended to Graham's head wound the police finally repulsed the demonstrators. The troops arrived and trotted slowly around the police cordon three or four times, then divided and paraded in two sections in opposite directions, passing each other on the north and south sides of the Square. In their glittering cuirasses and plumed helmets they evoked wild cheers from the spectators. At 4:14 P.M. a second reserve squadron arrived at Whitehall.

At ten minutes to five a battalion of Grenadier Guards, held in readiness at St. George's Barracks, marched into the Square shouldering rifles with fixed bayonets. They proceeded directly to the north side and vigorously drove the crowds back from the street, clearing the entire area in a most effective manner. Then they lined up in a double formation with fixed bayonets along the northern parapet. Shaw arrived at the Square in time to witness the dispersal:

> You should have seen that high-hearted host run. Running hardly expresses our collective action. We *skedaddled*, and never drew rein until we were safe on Hampstead Heath or thereabouts. Tarleton found me paralysed with terror, and brought me on to the square, the police kindly letting me through in consideration of my genteel appearance. On the whole I think it was the most abjectly disgraceful defeat ever suffered by a band of heroes outnumbering their foes a thousand to one....If Stead had not forced us to march on the Square a week too soon by his 'Not one Sunday must be allowed to pass' nonsense we should have been there now. It all comes from people trying to live down to fiction instead of up to facts.[30]

While the Guards were clearing the north area, one hundred police cavalry, wielding batons, dispersed the crowd on the south side. By 5:30 P.M. the worst danger had passed, and police and military remained in the Square only to clear the area of lingering spectators. At 6:30 the Life Guards marched a last time around the Square clearing all roadways and fifteen minutes later returned to their barracks. One small band of Grenadier Guards remained until 7:00 P.M. and then also departed. With a show of overwhelming force, Warren had made good his Trafalgar Square prohibition.

"Bloody Sunday" sent two hundred people to hospital, of whom two men subsequently died.[31] Seventy-seven constables sustained injuries, some with broken noses, and bitten fingers; others suffering blows from weapons as varied as belt buckles, truncheons and even life preservers. One policeman was trampled by a horse. Most of the injuries occurred between three and five o'clock in areas adjacent to the Square.[32]

Police arrested forty rioters mostly for personal assault. In Charing Cross a man named Sullivan knocked down a policeman with a brass ferruled stick. He was given six months hard labor. A Joseph Ellis was charged with striking a constable in the face with "a handkerchief containing some hard substance" and received eight months hard labor. George Harrison was sentenced to five years imprisonment for stabbing a policeman. Most others received summary sentences at Bow Court of from one to six months at hard labor. Burns and Graham were remanded for trial the following year on multiple charges.[33]

As always, the conduct of the police became a question of keen controversy. While many commended the police for their patience, seventy-five charges of brutality were lodged against constables by citizens. The *Pall Mall Gazette* titled its account of the affair "Bloody Sunday." Alleged eyewitnesses recalled widely conflicting accounts of the mélee, not surprising in view of the numbers involved and the innumerable clashes that were occurring simultaneously throughout the late afternoon.

Stead wrote to Gladstone that the action of the police "...was characterized by a brutality which I have never before seen in the whole of my life; and the sentences of three and six months, which have been passed upon men who provoked beyond endurance, struck back at their lawless assailants in uniform are simply infamous."[34]

By far the vast majority of people present in the streets adjoining the Square that day were spectators rather than demonstrators. The following recollection by Edward Carpenter, Labourite author (*Towards Democracy*), though by no means unbiased, suggests a bystander's point of view:

> Indeed, indeed though a large crowd it was of a most good-humored and peaceable kind; but the way in which it was 'worked up,' provoked and irritated by the police, was a caution; and gave me the strongest impression that this was done purposely, with the intention of leading to a collision.
>
> The order had gone forth we were to be 'kept moving.' ...We found ourselves violently pushed about by mounted and foot police and told to 'move on.' Whether Muirhead [Robert Muirhead, Carpenter's companion] did not move on fast enough, or what the trouble was, was never explained but the next moment I saw him seized by the collar by a mounted man and dragged along, apparently to a police station, while a bobby on foot aided in the arrest. I jumped to the rescue and slanged the two constables, for which I got a whack on the cheekbone from a baton...but Muirhead was released, and we soon regained our footing on the refuge, [a pedestrian island] from which for some time we watched the police continuing, at considerable risk to life and limb, to circle round and insult the 'mob.' One or two ugly rushes I believe and a few broken heads; but the damage of 'Bloody Sunday' did not after all amount to much.[35]

Among Burns' papers at the British Museum is an unsigned statement of another eyewitness apparently intended to be offered in evidence. The unknown spectator allegedly witnessed the most heated clash from a bus stalled in the very center of the action. His remarkable story:

It was a little after two O.C. when I arrived in the square. At first I took my stand on the steps of Morley's Hotel but after half an hour or so things became so exciting that I went down to the corner of the Strand to see the fun? Or was it that I myself was caught up in the enthusiasm of the hour? At any rate the processions were just then in full swing from every part and the police began to feel it hot. I may mention one thing that attracted me very much. Nearly all the fellows had little switches in their hands and partly in joke and maybe too in earnest here and there and over yonder they give a slight touch on the nose to the policemen's horses; they backed, they reared, they turned into each other, they bounded up. Certainly the police proved how well trained they had been in the riding school and being a farmer's son and had myself when a boy known something about riding a horse, I cannot tell how interested and pleased [I was] at such fine feats in riding. But on the crowds came in their thousands and soon I found the corner of the Strand was not a very pleasant spot to occupy. It was in that moment I discovered I had a Napoleonic genius. I went up to Charing Cross Station and took a bus to Piccadilly, got off at Piccadilly, back to Charing Cross and it was only on my third peregrination to Piccadilly that what I foresaw came to pass. The bus was stopped just about three perches from the Strand, and all the excited crowd were swaying to and fro around me. Now there were cries of excitement now low angry voices as the policemen jammed them back to keep the square free. It was then that I saw it and understood it. It was a *wedge* form[ed] of fellows determined and resolved. You [Burns] and Cunningham Graham were in the front. Just one press onward hardly without stirring foot—the first cordon of police were broken through, the second was broken through. Cries and shouts and through the third cordon had broken [sic]. The police in the front and those behind and scattered through the crowd were using their truncheons. I saw you and Graham brought out. His head was bleeding fearfully. It was just then that I saw the Horse Guards march up to the West End of the Square and began to walk very slowly round. I do not know how it happened but it was just from the very spot where I was placed I heard the officer give a command. The soldiers began to walk at a much quicker pace. All around from every part of the square the booing and the screaming was fearful. Again at the very same spot he gave another command and they began to trot. The screams and the shrieks that I then heard were in my ears for months. Again at the same spot he gave command. It was a wild cavalry charge around the square. The panic-stricken people tried to get away but loud above the clattering of the horses' hoofs and the rattling of their accoutrements were the frightened mad screams of the poor people. The square was now thinned indeed and I got down from the bus and with a heavy heart hurried away as quickly as I could for home.[36]

The Bermondsey Gladstone Club charged "...cowardly and murderous action of the Police in unjustifiably assaulting...peaceful and lawabiding citizens...."[37] But Gladstone himself, fearing that strong adverse reaction to the disorders might compromise also the Irish cause, wrote immediately to the Bermondsey Club "...that this question of Trafalgar Square meetings in all its phases should not be too closely allied with the Irish question."[38]

For his many Liberal supporters, Gladstone made his position perfectly clear:

> 'To anyone, whom my voice can reach, I would address the most urgent appeal to abstain from all countenance of violence, most of all in connection with the purpose which was announced yesterday.' The Irish cause would...'suffer disastrous prejudice were it to be associated in any manner with those who make appeals with Metropolitan disorder.'[39]

In the face of such statements by Gladstone, many of the Liberal groups associated in the Sunday march withdrew their support for the Trafalgar Square cause.

The socialists' cause suffered a great loss of public good will on account of their recourse to violence. An article in *The Contemporary Review* regretted that "the suffering that exists among the deserving poor has been used by political factions to set at defiance the officers of the law,..."[40] *The Times* had deplored the demonstrations from the very start, disbelieving that the leadership represented at all the legitimate "seekers after work."[41] The *Standard* refused to recognize any issue of the right of public meeting, and the *Globe* viewed that issue as only "a pretext for creating popular fermentation," and "a reign of terror and liberty to plunder and destroy."[42] Even the Liberal organ, the *Daily News*, while applauding the avowed object of the demonstration in regard to protesting O'Brien's imprisonment, contended that the right of public meeting was not at stake, and on the evening before the riot, decried the proposed demonstration.[43] Only the *Pall Mall Gazette* fully supported the demonstrators, Bradlaugh contributing a scathing denunciation of the police action. Hamilton considered the *Gazette's* position very much exaggerated: "There were no doubt a good many heads broken and the police appeared to have conducted themselves with some brutality, but nothing occurred to warrant the appellation 'Bloody Sunday.'"[44]

When the socialists announced plans to attempt another meeting in Trafalgar Square on the next Sunday, November 20, Warren expanded his unconditional ban on all meetings in or adjacent to the Square:

> Whereas the holding of meetings and the passages of processions have caused and are liable to cause public tumult and disorder in Trafalgar Square,...no meeting will be allowed to assemble, nor shall any person be allowed to deliver a public speech in Trafalgar Square, or in the streets or thoroughfares adjoining or leading thereto.
>
> No organized procession shall be allowed to pass along the streets or thoroughfares adjacent or leading to Trafalgar Square.[45]

To back up his ban, Warren advertised for thirty thousand volunteers to act as special constables on November 20, but this time the socialists backed down and shifted their meeting to Hyde Park. The demonstration there passed off without incident. Hamilton thought the seven thousand special constables who volunteered "appear to have had a very dreary day of it, pacing round Trafalgar Square, and to have considered that they were made rather fools of."[46]

Meanwhile Burns and Graham were released on bond, Burns' paid by Headlam and Graham's paid by Haldane.

Warren's sudden firmness ingratiated the police with the permanent residents and merchants of the area. Notes of support flooded Scotland Yard and the Home Office, and on subsequent weekends, a more tangible evidence of appreciation appeared in gifts of provisions and refreshments for the police patrols. Coffee and sandwiches were offered the men outside St. Stephen's Club and St. Martin's Church. Mrs. Hogg, "a well-known friend of the police," served at Queen Anne's Gate. A large hamper of provisions was delivered to Scotland Yard by a servant of a South Kensington resident. A Lavender Hill baker sent 120 loaves of bread, a Dr. Hison sixty meat pies. The only offering kindly refused was "...a van-load of cordials...to distribute in small glasses" suggested by a Mr. Christie.[47]

In defiance of Warren's ban and general public opinion the socialists persisted in their futile attempts to wear down the authorities and obtain the Square once more for demonstrations. To counter this, the Home Office and the police formulated a standing body of twenty thousand special constables who would be ready for duty any Sunday morning. The new group was placed under the command of Lt. Col. Daniell, Chief Constable of Hertfordshire. Each special was sworn in for two months possible duty, given a card and number, and assigned to an inspector in groups of one hundred. The force was then distributed throughout the Metropolitan area. They were not, however, to be called up without prior approval by the Home Secretary.[48]

On November 28 yet another socialist attempt to occupy the Square was repulsed but in the fighting one Alfred Linnell was badly injured and died several days later. His funeral on December 18 became the object of yet another demonstration, one of the largest in those years. The procession stretched out one and a half miles in length traversing Waterloo Street, the Strand, Fleet Street, St. Paul's, and Trafalgar Square of course, and terminating at Bow Cemetery. A black shield inscribed "Killed in Trafalgar Square" covered the coffin. Pall-bearers included Annie Besant, Cunninghame Graham, Stead and William Morris, who also composed the "death song" sung at the gravesite following the service performed by Headlam.[49]

Several days later police noticed a large placard with black borders at Clerkenwell Green which read:

Chief Bludgeoners, Brigands and Perjurers
Supt. Stied
Insp. Watts
Insp. Culmore

Another read;

Sacred to the memory of Alfred Linnell, basely and brutally murdered by order of Charles Warren, Chief Bludgeoner, Nov. 20, 1887.

Police asked the Home Office whether to prosecute for libel and Matthews requested a Legal Opinion on the matter. Poland recommended against prosecution of the case as too trivial.[50]

The much-publicized trial of Burns and Graham began on Monday, January 16 (1888). Graham was defended by his close friend Asquith, later the prime minister. Burns, "very hard up" financially, unable to face his landlord, defended himself "with vigor and adroitness," according to Asquith.[51] The chief prosecutor was Harry Bodkin Poland, one of the most feared prosecutors of his time, as is indicated by the grim parody of Campbell's famous lines of Kosciusko, "Poland, at whose name Freedom shrieks." He had served as legal counsel and prosecutor for the Treasury and the Home Office for the unequalled span of twenty-three years, participating in almost all the important criminal trials of his day. The attorney-general was Sir Richard Webster. The judge was Sir Arthur Charles, at forty-eight the youngest man on the Bench. He had only been appointed in September 1887, and the trial of Burns and Graham was one of his first. His cartoon appeared in *Vanity Fair* the month following the trial: "...like many other intelligent persons, he has a large nose."[52]

The government sought to prove that Warren's proclamation was entirely valid since the law gave control of Trafalgar Square to the police, who were fully empowered to regulate its use for the convenience of all citizens as a thoroughfare. The attorney-general argued that it was not only the right but the duty of the Metropolitan Police to prevent obstruction in a public place such as Trafalgar Square:

> The defendants were confusing the right of public meeting with the right of public discussion. No one denied that by the Law of England people might meet together and discuss public questions in a public hall or other places where they did not cause any obstruction. There was no doubt about the right of free discussion, it was a right of which the country was proud; but there was no right of holding a meeting anywhere just when a person liked. It had been held to be unlawful on the ground that it obstructed a thoughfare to exhibit pictures in a shop window, to place a chair or temporary erection in a street, to have a band, or to hold a pigeon match on private grounds so as to draw people together so as to cause an obstruction. There was no doubt about the right of public meeting, but it did not mean that a person had a right to hold a public meeting anywhere he liked.[53]

The government contended that the organizers ought to have held their meeting in Hyde Park when banned from the Square.

The Government's further contention was that Burns and Graham had led a charge with the *intention* of overpowering the police, and that the capture of the Square was foiled only because viciously armed supporters had been intercepted by extraordinary police preventive measures. As proof of this intention, the prosecution were able to place in evidence Graham's own statement made on the day in question. Graham had incautiously written to the *Pall Mall Gazette* from the police station complaining about the lack of support he and Burns had had in their attempt to hold the meeting. The case for the prosecution concluded with a grim recitation of the disorders occurring on November 13 and the injuries received by police on that day.

On the second day of the trial Burns, troubled by a headache and "not at all well in health," nevertheless conducted a very

spirited cross-examination of Warren and other prosecution witnesses.[54] In defense, Burns and Graham secured the friendly
testimony of a wide array of appropriately respectable witnesses,
engravers and engineers, Members of Parliament, a few anti-social-
ists, and even a Primrose Leaguer, all of whom dutifully testified
to the nonviolence of the defendants and the contrasting brutality
of the police. When Carpenter, the Labour leader from Sheffield,
was asked under cross-examination had he seen any rioting, "...I
replied in a very pointed way 'Not on the part of the people!' A
large smile went round the Court and I was not plied with any
more questions."[55] Bradlaugh, affirming, characterized Graham
and Burns as "hapless unfortunates in the hands of the police,"
and argued that he had conducted thirty or more public meetings
in Trafalgar Square over a period of as many years, never once
having been prohibited from doing so. Bradlaugh had not attended
the November 13 demonstration—he was lecturing at West Hartle-
pool—admitting that he rarely attended any out-door meetings "...
except those convened by himself."[56]

The testimony of only two defense witnesses proved unfortu-
nately damaging. James Tims, Secretary of the Radical Federation,
spent much of his time dissociating the radical movement from
that of the defendants. Hyndman's ill-advised and gratuitous
reference to the Pall Mall incident proved most damaging, and over
Burns' objections the prosecution were able to recount for the
jury in a very pejorative fashion the roles played by Burns and
Hyndman on that occasion.

Burns spoke in his own defense deriding the notion of armed
assault when his only weapons were "a pocket handkerchief and
a tramway ticket."[57] Asquith summed up for the Defense with a
legal characterization of the proposed Trafalgar Square demonstration as a lawful assembly and made persuasive reference to Beatty
vs. Gilbanks (see Chapter VI). If the meeting had not been prevented by police, he argued, there would have been no disorder.
The meeting being a lawful one, Warren's ban was invalid. As for
the composition and temperament of the crowd:

> It was an ordinary London crowd which, if not interfered with and
> allowed to go its own way, would behave in a perfectly proper and law-
> abiding manner....The conclusion which he invited the jury to come
> to as a fair result of the evidence was that Mr. Graham and Mr. Burns

were going unarmed and peaceably to assert what they believed to be the right of meeting in Trafalgar Square, that the police lost their heads, dashed upon them, and provoked a conflict which, but for the misguided action of the police, would not have occurred.[58]

The jury, which Burns later painted as "ten Tories, one liberal, and one radical" retired to consider its verdict late on the afternoon of January 18. "Never knew how much I loved till the interval between judge's summing up and return of the jury," as Burns himself described his feelings of anxiety and suspense. The jury took only slightly more than half an hour to convict the defendants on one count of unlawful assembly and acquit them of the more serious charges of riot and assault. Justice Charles sentenced both Burns and Graham to six months imprisonment without hard labor. "Pattie [Burns' wife] who had borne the ordeal very well seemed unusually cheerful. To make me feel less anxious whilst in prison she appeared as happy as possible. 'I would not love thee half so well loved I not honour more.' Goodbye, Pattie. The Warden beckons me." Ever dramatic, Burns thus described his and Graham's departure from the Old Bailey. A police Black Maria carried them both directly across the city to Pentonville Prison in Clerkenwell. Upon their arrival at the prison, the two convicted men stripped, bathed, and changed to prison clothing. Burns had difficulty finding a prison cap large enough to fit: "Graham stuck one on the side of his head, it was a glengarry, and swaggered about looking like a picture."[59]

Burns admitted his treatment at Pentonville was "...pretty good—sent to prison in good health, in twelve days lost ten lbs." He complained about the prison cursing and the parson's preaching, and made notes about the odd characters he met there, "human spokes in the wheel of vice." On February 8 he celebrated the anniversary of the Pall Mall Affair by singing the "Marseillaise" and inscribing "Long Live Socialism" on his cell wall.[60] Graham also alluded to the grim food and the unavoidable preaching:

'The dull week over, oakum all duly picked, cells well swept out, the skilly and brown bread discussed...' comes the chapel service. 'Dearly beloved' seems a little forced, our daily skilly scarce a matter worth much thanks, the trespasses of others we forgave....At last, after the week's silence, the prisoners burst triumphantly into the hymn: The pent-up sound breaks forth like an earthquake; the chapel quivers like a ship from stem to stern. And in the sounds the prison

melts away, the doors are opened and each man sits in his home surrounded by his friends, his Sunday dinner smokes, his children all clean
washed are on his side, and so we sing....[61]

The convictions caused considerable dismay among free speech
advocates. It was widely felt that the promoters had been in-
cautious and even irresponsible in challenging the government
under the circumstances which prevailed on November 13. Gladstone's opposition had already drained away much Liberal support,
and the convictions served to further dissuade others.

Bradlaugh, who placed much of the blame on Hyndman's poor
performance during cross-examination, also admitted the agitators
had chosen their ground inadvisedly. Even Asquith admitted some
years later that the practice of assembling a crowd, "...composed
for the most part, of idle and unemployed people, in and about
the Square, on any day and at any hour, under the guise of holding
a 'meeting,' had degenerated into an intolerable nuisance."[62] Even
such journals as the *Daily Chronicle* and *Daily News* urged the
cessation of the Trafalgar Square agitation.

In the House discussion of the matter, Bradlaugh and Sir Charles
Russell, the reluctant prosecutor of the Pall Mall conspirators, led
the attack. Sir Richard Webster, the Conservative Attorney General, defended the Government position.[63]

Upon release, Burns and Graham received each a hero's welcome
from supporters, including banquets and processions. On the
evening of his release Burns appeared as the guest of honor at a
reception held by Annie Besant's Law and Liberty League. Stead
presided. Burns was in a defiant mood:

> He was ashamed and disgusted with his own class. They were not
> educated as they ought to be, and a great deal of that was owing to
> their own apathy and indifference....Both himself and Mr. Graham
> pledged themselves to get into Trafalgar Square and speak or suffer
> the consequences and had ten thousand other men followed their
> example they would have gone through the cordon of police like a
> dose of salts, and with precisely the same result....They wanted a
> rallying cry as they wanted in Paris a hundred years ago....They chose
> the Bastille...and they whom he now addressed could make Trafalgar
> Square their revolutionary square and let the Bastille be Pentonville
> Prison, and when they had captured Trafalgar Square—and he intended
> to be one of those to do it—let the celebration of...their Trafalgar
> Square revolution be the demolition of the Bastille, that cursed prison
> at Pentonville which represented all the vices and the embodiment
> of all that was bad in the worst possible forms of government and the
> system of society.[64]

Burns' Bastille speech caused considerable consternation among the more moderate. Burns conceded in his diary that it had "frightened the weak-kneed liberals and irritated the rose-water revolutionists."[65] Michael Davitt attacked him two days later in another meeting.

Increasingly the flaming oratory of the agitators fell on deaf ears. Chiefly responsible was a quickening of the economy caused by a suddenly increased output of gold at the Rand mines in South Africa late in 1887. Exports rose gradually, unemployment dropped, and industrial production increased. The enthusiasn for further demonstrations flagged, and although Burns maintained for a time a breakneck pace of meeting after meeting, he had to concede less and less success. By April following a lackluster response to a Sunday morning speech to Wandsworth workers he admitted in his diary: "It requires a terrific amount of energy to rouse them from their apathy." By May he "...felt very depressed about the immediate future of the movement....We have dissipated nearly all our energy in the wrong direction upon the wrong men." Their inclination to rowdyism annoyed him more and more: "They seem more interested in a row than anything that benefits them."[66] Burns' growing disillusionment with the working class stemmed largely from the summer experience of 1888.

Frustrated by the improving economy and the concomitant growth of apathy among the workers, the agitators fell to squabbling among themselves. Shaw charged that Hyndman and Morris "...let the movement [SDF] go all to pieces by playing at soldiers with it. The Federation has gone to Hell, there is no Federation. The League has gone to Satan, there is no League, there is nothing but a Hammersmith Club and a Bloomsbury Club in the houses of which a handfull of idiots and anarchists fight once a week."[67] Burns attacked Hyndman for cowardice, claiming he had "...run from Trafalgar Square like a beaten cur...." For his part Hyndman derided Burns' "colossal conceit," and later labelled him a betrayer.[68] When Hyndman attacked Champion later in the year, Burns wrote in his diary: "From tonight dates the public downfall of a man [Hyndman] who has never lost an opportunity of showing his jealousy, proving his cowardice and proclaiming himself a skunk."[69] The estrangement of the old comrades was complete.

Lackluster attempts to re-open Trafalgar Square for meetings persisted throughout the summer of 1888, the agitators massing for "conversations" without actually holding meetings. Although no arrests were made on the grounds of illegal meetings, police dispersed all large gatherings in the Square as a matter of course. Mr. Conybeare (M.P. for Cornwall) compared the Police to Bashi-Bazouks and Matthews regretted that some M.P.s who ought to know better acted as "ringleaders" in these sorry affairs.[70]

Later in the year an opposition bill was brought before the House which would permit Trafalgar Square meetings. Still in the thick of the battle, Graham demanded angrily whether the Government "contemplates with much satisfaction a repetition of the Peterloo massacre?" The bill was lost.

In March 1889, John Burns was elected to the London County Council where he was later to relish welcoming as colleague none other than his earlier prosecutor Sir Harry Poland. Burns was one of Ben Tillett's chief aides in the extraordinary well-run (and successful) London docker's strike later in 1889. He entered Commons in 1892 and joined the Liberal Government of Campbell-Bannerman in 1905 as president of the Local Government Board. For many of his more radical former comrades he became "Labour's Lost Leader." His transformation is exemplified by the approving letter he received from Margot Asquith in 1906:

> I think you have...[set] an example of *moderation*—...moderation begets judgement [sic] and judgement honor. Violence and all such abuse is *such* a mistake...I congratulate you on your firm attitude towards the unemployed I know them well!...such rotters as most of them are....[71]

Though attacks on Trafalgar Square continued intermittently during the next several years, firm police policy prevented any outbreak as serious as that of Bloody Sunday, 1887. Sir Charles Warren resigned in 1888 and was succeeded by John Monro, who initiated a policy so repressive that even Matthews protested. Monro, exasperated by the pressure brought to bear on police by the increasing numbers of parades, demonstrations, and open-air rallies, convinced himself that since all processions and meetings caused some inconvenience to the public, they could all be prohibited on this ground. Placing great reliance on Warren's successfully upheld ban on Trafalgar Square,

Monro applied the same principle to virtually *all* demonstrations on a routine basis.

Since Matthews chivalrously defended the Commissioner in public, few people at the time were aware to what extent Matthews fought behind the scenes to moderate Monro's policies. He wrote in May of 1890 regarding Monro's ban of a Friendly Societies' parade:

> These men are the pick of the working classes, perfectly orderly, with an excellent object in view. It would be disastrous to get the police into collision with them. Processions are *not* necessarily illegal....
>
> I am quite aware how troublesome to the police these demonstrations are, but it will not do to go beyond the law in dealing with them. In the case of Trafalgar Square the law was strained to the utmost; but public safety and public opinion supported the action of the Police. That would not be so in this instance.[72]

Matthews' frequent over-rulings of Monro's actions strained relations to the utmost. In May 1890, someone leaked word of the internal dispute to the *Daily Telegraph* which immediately took Monro's part, whose policies it described as "crowned with success" up to now. "How can we answer the Socialists if they demand that what is sauce for the philanthropic goose should be sauce for the revolutionary gander."[73] At the Home Office a hunt was mounted for the informer without success. The running battle continued until the Conservatives left office in 1892.

Upon Gladstone's fourth and final return to office, Asquith received the Home Office. Within two days the Trafalgar Square issue reached his desk. It was a foregone assumption that the Conservative ban would be moderated in some way and Asquith was open to compromise. He sought the advice of Harcourt, then Chancellor of the Exchequer: "I don't want to seem to have my hand forced in this matter, and as we all know the ins and outs of it, I think it would be well before there is any agitation or pressure to announce a decision." Asquith hinted at a resumption of meetings on a limited basis.[74] Harcourt replied:

> The Trafalgar Square meeting is not [sic] doubt a serious business. In my time Bradlaugh held meetings there without any serious consequences. The affair in Childers' time in 1886 was a case of surprise which might and ought to have been prevented but of course it has left behind it a bad impression...If by taking proper precautions all fear of riot and serious obstruction of the traffic can be prevented I should certainly be in favor of allowing the meetings.[75]

Lifting the absolute ban, Asquith issued new regulations which permitted daylight meetings on Saturdays, Sundays and Bank Holidays provided police were given notice and approach routes approved. The limited right of meeting in Trafalgar Square met with approval from virtually all sides. Rosebery exulted that: "...To have pleased *The Times* and *The Star* and indeed everybody may rank with the achievements of Hannibal in crossing the Alps or of Orpheus charming his miscellaneous congregation."[76] Only Hyndman on the left and the Queen on the right disapproved and the latter told Asquith so. Harcourt welcomed it as a good sign, though warning his friend half in jest: "Woe unto them of whom *The Times* speaks well."[77] Asquith agreed: "When I read the *Times* article, I began to have an uneasy feeling that I must have made an ass of myself. Time will show."[78]

It was the Social Democrats who, on November 5, 1892, held the first meeting authorized by the new regulations. The following weekend, the fifth anniversary of Bloody Sunday, Burns spoke to a large audience: "...where five years ago Graham and I were beaten by the police."[79] The rules instituted by Asquith have remained in force ever since. And so at long last the thorny question of Trafalgar Square was laid to rest.

1. Hamilton Papers, B.M. Add. Mss. 48643, Diary for June 1887, f 66-77.

2. P.R.O. MEPOL/2/181.

3. William Booth, *Darkest England and the Way Out*, p. 100; *3 Hansard* CCCXX (1887). 727 ff. On November 16, 1887 *The Globe* reported statistics compiled by the Local Government Board: 100,244 Londoners chargeable to the rates, including 39,161 outdoor paupers and 1,013 vagrants.

4. G.D.H. Cole, *John Burns*, p. 14.

5. Dona Torr, *Tom Mann and His Times*, p. 259.

6. *The Times*, 1, 3, and 4 November 1887; *Annual Register* (1887), 158, and Part II, 49-51.

7. Burns Papers, B.M. Add. Mss. 46288, f 56.

8. Statement sworn by Mr. Francis Edwin Essington Farebrother, P.R.O. MEPOL/2/181.

9. *Dublin Review* (April 1906) as quoted in D.N.B.

10. Hamilton Papers, B.M. Add. Mss. 48645, Diary for December 6, 1886, f 47-48.

11. Hamilton Papers, 48646, Diary for July 5, 1887, f 90.

12. Salisbury papers, Matthews to Salisbury, October 22, 1887, E/4/87.

13. *The Times Law Review*, testimony given at Queen vs. Graham and Burns, January 17, 1888, p. 217 (hereafter referred to as Queen vs. Graham and Burns).

14. Warren to Matthews, October 31, 1887, P.R.O. MEPOL/2/182.

15. *The Times*, November 3 and 4, 1887.

16. Hamilton Papers, B.M. Add. Mss. 48647, 54, Diary for November 2, 1887.

17. *The Times*, November 5 and 8, 1887; Torr, p. 259.

18. The arrested journalists were Bennett Burleigh and A.F. Winkes. *The Times*, November 9, 1887.

19. P.R.O. MEPOL/2/182.

20. *The Times*, November 14, 1887.

21. Burgess, p. 100.

22. Great Britain, *Parliamentary Papers*, Vol. LXI (1889), "Trafalgar Square Regulations."

23. Queen vs. Graham and Burns, 219.

24. John Mackail, *Life of William Morris*, II p. 191.

25. Thomas Lloyd Humberstone, *Commemoration of the Sixtieth Anniversary of the "Battle of Trafalgar Square,"* p. 14.

26. Queen vs. Graham and Burns, 216 ff.

27. *The Times*, November 14, 1887.

28. Queen vs. Graham and Burns, 212.

29. Burgess, p. 101.

30. Quoted in Kent, 30.

31. Torr, p. 343; *Annual Register* (1887), 176.

32. Great Britain, *Parliamentary Papers*, Vol. LXXXII (1888), "Return of Policemen Injured on the 19th day of November, 1887, giving the Name, Rank, and Number of the Persons Injured, the Nature of the Injury, and the Time and Place at which it was Sustained."

33. P.R.O. MEPOL/2/182.

34. Stead to Gladstone, November 14, 1887, Gladstone Papers, B.M. Add. Mss. 44303 f 378-9.

35. Edward Carpenter, *My Days and Dreams*, pp. 254-6.

36. Burns Papers, B.M. Add. Mss. 46288, 53-55.

37. Gladstone Papers, B.M. Add. Mss. 44502, f 100-101.

38. Gladstone to Secretary of Bermondsey Gladstone Club, November 14, 1887, Gladstone Papers, B.M. Add. Mss. 44502, f 106, 107.

39. Gladstone Papers, B.M. Add. Mss. 44502, f 102.

40. Francis Peek, "The Workless, the Thriftless, and the Worthless," *The Contemporary Review*, LIII (January 1888), 39.

41. *The Times*, November 9, 1887.

42. *Standard* (London), November 14, 1887; *The Globe*, November 17, 1887.

43. *London Daily News*, November 9 and 10, 1887.

44. Hamilton Papers, B.M. Add. Mss. 48647, Diary for November 18, 1887.

45. Great Britain, *Parliamentary Papers*, Vol. LXI (1889), "Trafalgar Square Regulations."

46. Hamilton Papers, B.M. Add. Mss. 48647, Diary for November 21, 1887; *Annual Register* (1887), 177.

47. P.R.O. MEPOL/2/182.

48. P.R.O. MEPOL/2/174.

49. Cole, *John Burns*, p. 15; Burgess, *John Burns*, p. 102.

50. P.R.O. MEPOL/2/182.

51. Burns Papers, B.M. Add. Mss. 46310, f 3-5, Diary for January 9-16, 1888; H.H. Asquith, *Memories and Reflections*, Vol. I p. 87.

52. *Vanity Fair*, February 4, 1888.

53. Queen vs. Graham and Burns, 212.

54. Burns Papers, B.M. Add. Mss. 46301, Diary for January 17, 1887.

55. Edward Carpenter, *My Days and Dreams*, p. 256.

56. Hypatia Bradlaugh Bonner and John M. Robertson, *Charles Bradlaugh*, Vol. II, p. 382-ff; Queen vs. Graham and Burns, 219; Kent, *John Burns*, p. 32.

57. G.H. Knott, *Mr. John Burns, M.P.*, p. 46.

58. Queen vs. Graham and Burns, 223.

59. Burns Papers, B.M. Add. Mss. 46305, f 26; 46310, f 3-5; 46308, f 43.

60. Burns Papers, B.M. Add. Mss. 46305, f 37; 46310, f 5.

61. Humberstone, p. 15.

62. Bonner and Robertson, 384; Asquith, I, 87-88.

63. *3 Hansard*, CCCXXIX (1888), 42 ff.

64. Kent, p. 32.

65. Burns Papers, B.M. Add. Mss. 46310 f 13.

66. Burns Papers, B.M. Add. Mss. 46310, Diary for April 15, 1888; May 10, 1888; May 13, 1888.

67. Shaw to Hyndman, June 22, 1888, Shaw Papers, B.M. Add. Mss. 50538, f 104.

68. Burgess, p. 189; viii.

69. Burns Papers, 46310, f 75, Diary for October 26, 1888.

70. *3 Hansard*, CCCXXVIII (1888), 1417-1422.

71. Margot Asquith to Burns, January 17, 1906, Burns Papers, 46282, f 39.

72. Matthews to Monro, May 3, 1890, P.R.O. MEPOL/2/248.

73. *Daily Telegraph*, May 10, 1890.

74. Asquith to Harcourt, August 21, 1892, Harcourt Papers.

75. Harcourt to Asquith, August 24, 1894, Harcourt Papers.

76. Jenkins, *Asquith*, 64-65.

77. Harcourt to Asquith, October 20, 1892, Harcourt Papers.

78. Asquith to Harcourt, October 21, 1892, Harcourt Papers.

79. Burns Papers, 46312, f 47, Diary for November 13, 1892.

10

CONCLUSION

One of the underlying premises of this book is that the widely-held belief in the public orderliness of Victorian society, at least in the eighteen-sixties, seventies, and eighties, is a gross misconception. The phenomenon of widespread crowd disturbances described here may help to dispel such a mistaken notion. Nor were the disorders examined in this work the only ones. Industrial disputes frequently involved serious rioting. The Welsh anti-tithe agitation became quite violent during the eighties. The Scottish crofters' and cottars' disturbances severely tested both police and military authority. There were many other religious lecturers in addition to William Murphy whose crusades invited serious mob attack. Orange processions invariably precipitated violent disturbances. Wherever crowds gathered, whether for political or religious reasons, public hangings, evictions, or sporting events, there was a serious threat to public order which required appropriate police response. Britain in the eighteen-sixties, seventies and eighties, contrary to popular belief, was in fact a very disorderly society.

Certainly it can hardly be denied that the crowd disorders delineated here may seem mild indeed when compared to the far more violent American or continental experience during the same period. To some the Victorian riots may seem perfectly innocuous in retrospect. The comparisons are not quite fair. One lives in one's own time and place and the Victorian perceptions of civil disorder must be accepted as genuine. The Victorian authorities viewed the dangers as quite real and the response was commensurate. It is quite likely that awareness of more serious riots elsewhere exacerbated their fears of domestic disturbances.

In retrospect however, the disorders do not seem to have posed any revolutionary threat. Nor did the disturbances bear the earmarks of agitations championing any serious political or social cause. The serious disorders which accompanied the crusade for the Reform Bill in 1831 had no counterpart even in 1848, a season of severe Continental upheavals. *The Times* was able to write with transparent relief: "The signal of unconstitutional menace, of violence, of insurrection, of revolution, was yesterday given in our streets, and happily despised by a peaceful, prudent, and loyal metropolis."[1] For the next two decades agitators mourned the general apathy of the British populace. Most of the crowds at Hyde Park in July, 1866, were spectators and curiosity-seekers, not rioters at all. On July 23, when the railing collapsed and the crowd swarmed through the park, many of those present were women, one actually carrying a baby in arms.[2] Karl Marx, in London at the time, wrote to Friedrich Engels that if only a few of the crowd had used the railings offensively against the police and killed some twenty, "then there would have been some fun."[3] Herman Ausubel concludes that far from being the result of popular pressure, the Bill of 1867 was actually passed in spite of a lack of public spirit.[4] Spencer Walpole, whose treatment of the 1866 riots is described by Trevelyan as the "best account," wrote of the apathy and complacency of the masses; Frances Gillespie, whose *Labour and Politics in England 1850-1867* treats the Hyde Park incident in great detail, concluded that British society of the sixties was characterized by complacency and inertia.[5] Such observations might be multiplied endlessly. All the evidence points to the good-natured spirit which seemed to prevail in crowd disturbances. Especially in gatherings where the right of public meeting had become an issue most demonstrators displayed a very real reluctance to challenge authority. If they did charge a police line, it was an almost amiable encounter, certainly not vicious. Much to the chagrin of the more extremist agitators, most crowds contained a great many fair-weather demonstrators who might just as easily raise a good-natured cheer for the police as mount a charge. As we have seen, London crowds frequently cheered even the military.[6]

Far from rioting seriously in behalf of political, social or economic reforms, the working classes incurred the almost universal accusation of indifference from professional agitators and would-be reform leaders. Tom Mann often expressed his exasperation at the various excuses he heard from workingmen who refused to join socialist or radical crusades.[7] Henry Hyndman wrote of the patient, long-suffering, and apathetic working classes during the eighties, and William Morris complained bitterly of the same thing.[8] The *Annual Register* described the state of public spirit during the seventies:

> Whatever signs there might be of disturbance of the present order of things, they denoted no immediate agitation. Changes and movements were talked of but prospectively. Indifference seemed to be more and more the leading characteristic of the bulk of the people—of the great body of the middle classes at all events—and political and social agitators strove in vain to strike a spark out of them, with any real flame in it, upon any subject whatever.[9]

As late as 1903 Keir Hardie deplored the "fatalistic patience" of the London unemployed, "these crowds of helpless atoms" who had no fight left in them.[10] *The Times* editorialized on the morrow of "Bloody Sunday":

> It was no enthusiasm for free speech, no reasoned belief in the innocence of Mr. O'Brien, no serious conviction of any kind, and no honest purpose that animated these howling roughs. It was simple love of disorder, hope of plunder, and the revolt of dull brutality against the rule of law.[11]

Discounting the pejorative insinuations expected in any *Times'* treatment of socialist or radical agitation, the editorial yet contained some keen insights.

It has frequently been remarked that the period was one notably deficient in public amusements. Cole and Postgate wrote of the narrowness and montony of Victorian urban working classes,[12] and Charles Booth concluded that a large part of the London disorderliness stemmed from a great dearth of recreational facilities for the working classes.[13] In the smaller towns and villages of the countryside, the monotony of life was even more oppressive than in the cities. In the sixties John Morley pointed out the "utter lack of means of amusement or moderate excitement" which prevailed in country towns, and deprecated the "sheer monotony and crushing dulness" of rural life.[14]

Although perhaps not currently a very fashionable suggestion, "simple love of disorder" may have played a far larger role than has been accorded to it. There is much Victorian evidence to support Robert Ardrey's "violence is fun" thesis. The magnetic attraction of excitement for its own sake cannot be minimized. For the laboring classes the prospect of an occasional happy relief from the dreary respectability of their pedestrian lives was too appealing to resist. The chances of being called to account for participation in such boisterous crowd outbursts were remote. The sound of shattered glass, the spectacle of police on the run, may have been intoxicating enough to explain the root cause of many Victorian civil disorders.[15]

Turning, then, from historical considerations for the moment, we may hope to benefit from the tenets of several schools of social psychology. The earliest approach to crowd behavior was essentially psychological, represented by Le Bon, Sighele, Tarde, Freud, Ross, Martin, et al. Most Victorian crowds fit Le Bon's concept of the "psychological crowd." Some of Le Bon's characteristics of crowds such as suggestibility, mobility, volatility, ingenuousness, tendency to self-justification, etc., apply easily. Others do not, most notably caprice, irrationality, and the capacity for savage irritability. British crowds perpetrated their property damage selectively, not indiscriminately; George Rudé has noticed a similar pattern in his study of the pre-industrial crowd in England and France.[16] British crowds engaged in little looting and although they rarely quailed at the prospect of a brawling mêlée, there was a conspicuous absence of mortalities. Much of Le Bon's emphasis on the irrationality of crowds derives from his premise of the "mental unity of crowds," now discredited by most social psychologists; his invariably pejorative view of crowds results from his cynical conservatism; and his emphasis on their savage capabilities is explained perhaps by his almost complete reliance on the French experience.

A second (and more recent) approach is essentially sociological. To students of "collective behavior" the riot is a "hostile outburst" and the determinants are structural conduciveness, strain, generalized hostile beliefs, precipitating factors, and mobilization. Social psychologists have noticed that once an outburst has commenced a generalized tendency to defy authority spreads rapidly, accompanied by the attraction of individual delinquents of all sorts whose presence tends to increase the disorder.[17]

Most historians have taken scant account of the social psychologists, even when dealing with crowd phenomena, perhaps due to the sociologists' seeming proclivity for endless terminological proliferation, the anti-historical bias of Le Bon, and a share of professional narrowmindedness. But some scholars have been examining the crowd from below, not as a psychological unity or a sociological abstraction to be lauded as *le peuple* or denigrated as *la canaille*, but as assemblage of individuals, each with his own distinct set of motivations and goals. The research techniques employed by Lefebvre, Soboul, Rudé, Chevalier, Pinkney and others in determining the composition of French revolutionary crowds have proved quite worthwhile and should suggest further understandings of the British crowd.

The major focus of this study has not been the rioters, but the forces of riot control: the police, the military, and most especially the Home Office. The repressive forces at the disposal of Victorian authority have been shown to be at best embryonic. It seems clear that whatever order did prevail was due as much to crowd restraint as to police effectiveness. Unarmed police were invariably outnumbered by the crowds they faced and the use of the special constables was not really effective. Deployment of the military was a last resort, and one fraught with a tangle of legal and emotional difficulties. Victorian authority thus relied quite heavily on the ultimate good sense of the citizen body, a confidence frequently expressed by officials in times of crisis.

The panic caused by Fenian terrorism was perceived correctly as a danger of a more serious nature than disorderly crowds, and authorities might have been excused had they over-reacted under the circumstances. In spite of police inefficiency and real bungling, however, the Home Office muddled through the crisis without resorting to measures of repression which would have truly compromised citizens' liberties. Fortunately so, for had this brief exposure to terrorism had a less happy conclusion, the retention of an unarmed police force would have been much sooner at issue.

Far less dangerous to the Government, but no less incendiary on another level were the crusades of William Murphy, the Salvation Army, and other religious lecturers. Their methods and messages evoked the worst in Victorian sentiments and crowd behavior. Local authorities, and ultimately the Home Office, found themselves in the familiar but no less frustrating position of extending protection to individuals and causes with which they had no sympathy whatever. For their part, most of the crusaders studied here defied all reasonable restraint and seemed determined to flaunt their views in the face of acknowledged community hostility. Not surprisingly, local authorities showed themselves quite susceptible to local pressures.

The Home Office might be expected to take a wider view. Both Hardy and Bruce personally considered Murphy a downright nuisance and incendiary. Both probed legal avenues of suppression. Finding none, Hardy acquiesced and insisted on a strict administration of the demands of the law while assuaging his conscience by attempting to moderate animosities as much as possible. Bruce, on the other hand, could not find it within himself to extend the legal protection of the Home Office to a man he despised as an outright scoundrel, and deployed every obstacle he could in Murphy's path. Harcourt found himself in a similar position *vis-a-vis* the Salvation Army. Although in every other circumstance an ardent civil libertarian, Harcourt's actions with regard to the very unpopular Salvation Army were extremely unsympathetic until reversed by judicial decision.

It was in the continuing clashes over the right of public meeting and right to assembly that the sagacity of the Home Secretaries was most keenly tested. Faced by demands for protection of demonstrations from republicans, socialists, radicals, unemployed, and a myriad number of other groups, the Home Office was repeatedly challenged to render the most delicate decisions. Preservation of public order had to be balanced against the competing need to assure the traditional British right of public meeting. Walpole's utter disgrace in 1867 shows the inevitable consequences of the slightest miscalculation. Childers escaped a similar fate following the Pall Mall Affair in 1886 only because he had just taken office the day of the riot and because most of the blame was directed at the Superintendent of Police.

All things considered, the record of the Victorian Home Office was not a poor one. In difficult times, the Home Secretaries acted with a restraint which far exceeded that of lower officials and resisted overreaction to crises. The correspondence clearly shows the conscientious wrestling with the issues which preceded decisions and sincere desire to find the fairest and most morally appropriate response to a given dilemma. There is no evidence of heavy-handed abuse of powers or, on the other hand, undue truckling to popular pressure. It was not a perfect record, but commendable enough so that it may not be too much to say the performance of the Home Office constituted one of the triumphs of Victorian bureaucracy.

1. *The Times*, April 11, 1848.
2. Spencer Walpole, *The History of Twenty-Five Years*, II, p. 174.
3. Asa Briggs, *Victorian People*, p. 206.
4. Herman Ausubel, *In Hard Times*, p. 9.
5. Walpole, p. 160; Frances Gillespie, *Labor and Politics in England 1850-1867*, pp. 235, 268. For a dissenting view, see Royden Harrison, *Before the Socialists*.
6. See especially Chapters VIII and IX.
7. Dona Torr, *Tom Mann and His Times*, I, p. 189.
8. Henry Hyndman, "The English Workers as They are," *The Contemporary Review*, LII, 135, 136; John Mackail, *Life of William Morris*, II, 156. See also G.D.H. Cole and Raymond Postgate, *The British Common People 1746-1938*, p. 389.
9. *Annual Register* (1872), p. 8.
10. William Stewart, *J. Keir Hardie*, p. 197.
11. *The Times*, November 14, 1887.
12. Cole and Postgate, p. 339.
13. Charles Booth, *Life and Labour of the People in London*, XVII, 52.
14. John Morley, *Studies in Conduct*, pp. 223, 226.
15. The present author has categorized 452 riotous disturbances during the period 1865-1914; unpublished dissertation "Public Order and Popular Disturbances in Great Britain 1865-1914," University of Maryland, 1964.
16. The only exception noticed was a disturbance at Leamington in which the rioters destroyed property allegedly irrespective of party considerations (Saunders, p. 231). See Rudé, pp. 253 ff.
17. Neil J. Smelser, *Theory of Collective Behavior* (1963), pp. 256-258.

BIBLIOGRAPHY

PERSONAL PAPERS

Aberdare Papers, in Lord Aberdare's possession.
Asquith Papers, Bodleian Library.
Burns Papers, British Museum.
Cairns Papers, Public Record Office.
Childers Papers, Royal Commonwealth Society.
Cranbrook Papers, Ipswich and East Suffolk Record Office.
Cross Papers, British Museum.
Disraeli Papers, Hughenden Manor.
Ellenborough Papers, Public Record Office.
Gladstone Papers, British Museum.
Hamilton Papers, British Museum.
Harcourt Papers, Stanton Harcourt, in Lord Harcourt's possession.
Mayo Papers, British Museum.
Milner Papers, Bodleian Library.
Russell Papers, Public Record Office.
Salisbury Papers, Christ Church.
Shaw Papers, British Museum.

OFFICIAL PAPERS

Great Britain. *Hansard's Parliamentary Debates* .
Great Britain. *Parliamentary Papers.* Vol. VIII. 1868–1869. "Report from the Select Committee on Parliamentary and Municipal Elections."
Great Britain. *Parliamentary Papers.* Vol. III. 1872. "Parks Regulation Act."
Great Britain. *Parliamentary Papers.* Vol. LXI. 1876. "Copy of Correspondence between Mr. Whalley, M.P., and the Secretary of State for the Home Department, in reference to Public Meetings held at Ipswich, Colchester, and Bury-St. Edmunds in October last."
Great Britain. *Parliamentary Papers.* Vol XIV. 1881. "Preliminary Report of the Royal Commission on Agriculture."
Great Britain. *Parliamentary Papers.* Vol XV. 1882. "Final Report of the Royal Commission on Agriculture."
Great Britain. *Parliamentary Papers.* Vol. LIX. 1882. "Deaths from Starvation (Metropolis)."
Great Britain. *Parliamentary Papers.* Vol. LIV. 1882. "Return containing Copies of any Correspondence which has passed between the Home Office and the Local Authorities of Basingstoke and other Places, with reference to the Suppression of Disturbances."

Great Britain. *Parliamentary Papers*. Vols. XXI-XXIII. 1886. "Final Report of the Royal Commission Appointed to Inquire into the Depression of Trade and Industry."

Great Britain. *Parliamentary Papers*. Vol. XXXIV. C. 4665. 1886. "Report of a Committee to inquire and report as to the Origin and Character of the Disturbance which took Place in the Metropolis on Monday, the 8th of February, and as to the Conduct of the Police Authorities in Relation Thereto; with Minutes of Evidence and Appendix."

Great Britain. *Parliamentary Papers*. Vol. XXXIV. 1886. "Police (Counties and Boroughs), Reports of the Inspectors of Constabulary for the Year ending 29th September, 1885."

Great Britain. *Parliamentary Papers*. Vol. LXXXI. 1888. "Correspondence between the Secretary of State for the Home Department and the Metropolitan Board of Works, relating to the Right of Public Meeting in certain Open Spaces subject to the jurisdiction of the Board."

Great Britain. *Parliamentary Papers*. Vol. LXXXII. 1888. "Return of Policemen Injured on the 13th day of November, 1887, giving the Name, Rank, and Number of the Persons Injured, the Nature of the Injury, and the Time and Place at which it was Sustained."

Great Britain. *Parliamentary Papers*. Vol. LXXXII. 1888. "Return of Cost of Police in Boroughs of Great Britain over 100,000 Inhabitants."

Great Britain. *Parliamentary Papers*. Vol. LXI. 1889. "Trafalgar Square Regulations."

Great Britain. *Parliamentary Papers*. Vol. LXIII. 1890-1891. "Copy of Correspondence between the Secretary of State for the Home Department and the Northampton Magistrates with reference to the Prohibition of a Meeting intended to have been held in the Market Square, Northampton."

Great Britain. *Parliamentary Papers*. Vol. LXV. 1892. "Metropolitan Police District (Open Air Meetings)."

Great Britain. *Parliamentary Papers*. Vol. LXV. 1892. "Eastbourne Improvement Act, 1885 (Prosecutions for Open-air Services, etc.)."

Great Britain. *Parliamentary Papers*. Vol. XXXIX. 1893. "Royal Commission on Labour: Minutes of Evidence with the Fourth Report."

Great Britain. *Parliamentary Papers*. Vol. XVI. 1894. "Reports of the Royal Commission on Agriculture."

Great Britain. *Parliamentary Papers*. Vol. VIII. 1895. "Reports of the Select Committee on Distress from Want of Employment."

Great Britain. *Parliamentary Papers*. Vol. XXXV. C. 7650. 1895. "Report of the Interdepartmental Committee on Riots appointed by the Home Secretary May 1894."

Great Britain. *Parliamentary Papers*. Vol. LXXVI. C. 8211. 1896. "Statistical Tables showing the progress of British Trade and Production 1854-95."

Great Britain. *Parliamentary Papers*. Cd. 1761. 1903. "Memoranda, Statistical Tables, and Charts prepared in the Board of Trade with reference to various matters on British and Foreign Trade and Industrial Conditions."

Great Britain. *Parliamentary Papers*. Vol. CIII. 1906. "Report of the Departmental Committee on Vagrancy."

Great Britain. *Parliamentary Papers*. Vol. VII. 1908. "Report of the Select Committee on the Employment of Military in Cases of Disturbances."

Great Britain. *Parliamentary Papers.* Vol. XXXVI. 1909. "Report of the Departmental Committee on the Duties of the Police with respect to the Preservation of Order at Public Meetings."

NEWSPAPERS

Birmingham Daily Post.
Cornish Telegram.
Daily Chronicle (London).
Daily Telegraph (London).
The Globe (London).
Graphic (London).
Leeds Mercury.
London Daily News.
Morning Herald (London).
Morning Post (Birmingham).
Morning Post (London).
North British Daily Mail.
Pall Mall Gazette (London).
Reynold's (London).
Standard (London).
Sunderland Herald.
The Times (London).
West Sussex Gazette.
Whitehaven Herald.

PERIODICALS

Annual Register.
Commonweal.
Constitutional Year Book.
The Contemporary Review.
The Economist.
The Fortnightly Review.
The Law Journal.
The National Review.
The New Review.
The Nineteenth Century.
The Quarterly Review.
Saturday Review.
The Spectator.
The Syndicalist.

BOOKS AND ARTICLES

Albery, William. *A Parliamentary History of the Ancient Borough of Horsham, 1295-1885.* London, 1927.

Altick, Richard D. *Victorian People and Ideas.* New York, 1973.

Appleman, P., Madden, W., and Wolff, M. (eds.). *1859: Entering an Age of Crisis.* Bloomington, Indiana, 1959.

Arch, Joseph, *The Story of His Life Told by Himself.* London, 1898.

Ashby, Mabel. *Joseph Ashby of Tysoe 1859-1919: A Study of English Village Life.* London, 1961.

Asquith, H.H. *Fifty Years of Parliament.* 2 Vols. London, 1926.

———. *Memories and Reflections.* 2 Vols. London, 1928.

Ausubel, Herman. *In Hard Times: Reformers Among the Late Victorians.* New York, 1960.

Barnett, Samuel A. "Distress in East London." *The Nineteenth Century,* XX (November, 1886), 679-692.

Beer, Max. *A History of British Socialism.* London, 1940.

Begbie, Harold. *The Life of General William Booth.* 2 Vols. New York, 1920.

Beloff, Max. *Public Order and Disturbances 1660-1714.* Oxford, 1938.

Best, Geoffrey. *Mid-Victorian Britain: 1851-1875.* New York, 1972.

Blagg, J.W. *The Law As to Public Meetings.* London, 1888.

Bonner, Hypatia Bradlaugh, and Robertson, J.M. *Charles Bradlaugh.* 2 Vols. London, 1895.

Booth, Charles. *Life and Labour of the People in London.* 17 Vols. London, 1889-1903.

Booth, William. *In Darkest England and the Way Out.* London, 1890.

Borthwick, Algernon. "The Primrose League," *The Nineteenth Century,* XX (July, 1886), 33-39.

Bosanquet, Helen. *Social Work in London 1869-1912.* London, 1914.

Bowski, William M. "The Medieval Commune and Internal Violence: Police Power and Safety in Siena, 1287-1355," *American Historical Review,* LXXIII (October, 1967)

Briggs, Asa. *Victorian People.* London, 1954.

Bright, John. *The Diaries of John Bright.* Edited by R. Walling.

Brinton, Crane. *English Political Thought in the Nineteenth Century.* London, 1933.

Broadhurst, Henry. *Henry Broadhurst, M.P. The Story of His Life from a Stonemason's Bench to the Treasury Bench Told By Himself.* London, 1901.

Brownlie, Ian. *The Law Relating to Public Order.* London, 1968.

Bruce, H.A. *Letters and Addresses.* Privately printed, 1916.

———. *Letters of the Rt. Hon. Henry Austin Bruce.* Privately printed, 1902.

Buckle, George E. (ed.). *The Letters of Queen Victoria.* London, 1926-1932.

———, and Monypenny, William. *The Life of Benjamin Disraeli, Earl of Beaconsfield.* 2 Vols. New York, 1929.

Burgess, Joseph. *John Burns: The Rise and Progress of a Right Honorable.* Glasgow, 1911.

Burleigh, Bennet. "The Unemployed," *The Contemporary Review,* LII (December, 1887), 770-780.

Burns, John. "The Great Strike," *The New Review,* I (October, 1889), 410-422.

———. *The Man With the Red Flag. Being the speech delivered at the Old Bailey.* London, 1886.

Carpenter, Edward. *My Days and Dreams.* London, 1916.

Cecil, David. *Lord M.* London, 1954.

Chapman, Samuel G. (ed.). *The Police Heritage in England and America.* East Lansing, Michigan, 1962.

Childers, E.S.E. *The Life and Correspondence of the Rt. Hon. Hugh Culling Eardley Childers.* 2 Vols. London, 1901.

Clapham, John H. *An Economic History of Modern Britain.* 3 Vols. Cambridge, England, 1951-1952.

Clark, G. Kitson. *The Making of Victorian England.* London, 1962.

Clayden, Peter. *England Under Beaconsfield.* London, 1891.

_____. *England Under the Coalition.* London, 1892.

Clive, John. "British History, 1870-1914 Reconsidered: Recent Trends in the Historiography of the Period," *American Historical Review,* LXVIII (July, 1963), 987-10099.

Cole, G.D.H. *British Working Class Politics 1832-1914.* London, 1941.

_____. *John Burns.* London, 1943.

_____. *A Short History of the British Working Class Movements 1789-1947.* Revised. London, 1948.

_____, and Postgate, Raymond. *The British Common People 1746-1938.* New York, 1939.

Collier, Richard. *The General Next to God. The Story of William Booth and the Salvation Army.* London, 1965.

Cowling, Maurice. *1867: Disraeli, Gladstone and Revolution.* Cambridge, 1967.

Darvall, Frank O. *Popular Disturbances and Public Order in Regency England.* London, 1934.

Dicey, Albert. *Lectures on the Relation Between Law and Public Opinion in England During the Nineteenth Century.* London, 1905.

Disraeli, Benjamim. *Sibyl.* London, 1844.

Ensor, R.C.K. *England 1870-1914.* Vol. XIV of *The Oxford History of England.* Oxford, 1960.

Escott, Thomas. *England: Her People, Policy and Pursuits.* Revised. London, 1885.

The Fabian Society. *Fabian Tracts.* No. X. London, 1892.

Fay, Charles. *Life and Labour in the Nineteenth Century.* 4th ed. Cambridge, England, 1948.

Finer, H. "The Police and Public Safety," in *A Century of Municipal Progress 1835-1935.* Edited by Harold Laski, W. Jennings, and William Robson. London, 1935.

Fletcher, T.W. "The Great Depression of English Agriculture 1873-1896," *Economic History Review,* Second series, XIII, No. 3 (1961), 417-432.

Fredur, Thor [pseud.]. *Sketches from Shady Places.* London, 1879.

Gardiner, A.G. *The Life of Sir William Harcourt.* 2 Vols. London, 1923.

Garvin, James L. *Life of Joseph Chamberlain.* 4 Vols. London, 1932—.

Gash, Norman. *Politics in the Age of Peel.* London, 1953.

Gathorne-Hardy, Alfred E. *Gathorne-Hardy, 1st Earl Cranbrook, A Memoir.* London, 1910.

Gillespie, Frances. *Labor and Politics in England 1850-1867.* Durham, South Carolina, 1927.

Grego, Joseph. *History of Parliamentary Elections and Electioneering in the Old Days.* London, 1886.

Grubb, A.P. *John Burns*. London, 1908.

Gwyn, William. *Democracy and the Cost of Politics in Britain*. London, 1962.

Halevy, Elie. *A History of the English People in the Nineteenth Century*. Translated by E. Watkin and D. Barker. 6 Vols. New York, 1924-1951.

Hanham, H.G. *Elections and Party Management: Politics in the Time of Disraeli and Gladstone*. London, 1959.

Harrison, Royden. *Before the Socialists*. London, 1965.

Hart, Jenifer M. *The British Police*. London, 1951.

_____. "Reform of the Borough Police, 1835-1856," *English Historical Review*, LXX (1955), 411-427.

Hastings, Sydney. *Riots: A Concise Statement of the Common and Statute Law Relating Thereto*. London, 1886.

Himmelfarb, Gertrude. "The Politics of Democracy: The English Reform Act of 1867," *Journal of British Studies* (November, 1966).

Hobsbawm, Eric. *Labour's Turning Point. 1880-1900*. London, 1948.

_____. *Primitive Rebels*. Manchester, 1959.

Holmes, Thomas. *London's Underworld*. London, 1912.

Holyoake, George. *Sixty Years of an Agitator's Life*. 2 Vols. London, 1892.

Houghton, Walter E. *The Victorian Frame of Mind 1830-1870*. New Haven, 1957.

Howell George. *Labour Legislation Labour Movements and Labour Leaders*. London, 1902.

Humberstone, Thomas Lloyd. *Commemoration of the Sixtieth Anniversary of the "Battle of Trafalgar Square."* London, 1948.

Hyndman, Henry. "The Dawn of a Revolutionary Epoch," *The Nineteenth Century*, IX (January, 1881), 1-18.

_____. "The English Workers As they Are," *The Contemporary Review*, LII (July, 1887), 122-136.

_____. *Further Reminiscences*. London, 1912.

_____. *Record of an Adventuous Life*. New York, 1911.

Jackman, Sydney W. (ed.). *The English Reform Tradition 1790-1910*. Englewood Cliffs, New Jersey, 1967.

Jenkins, Roy. *Life of Asquith*. London, 1964.

Jones, Gareth Stedman. *Outcast London*. Oxford, 1971.

Kent, William. *John Burns: Labour's Lost Leader*. London, 1950.

Knott, G.H. *Mr. John Burns, M.P.* London, 1901.

Lambert, Brooke, "Esau's Cry," *The Contemporary Review*, XLIV (December, 1883), 916-923.

Lee, W.L. Melville. *History of Police in England*. London, 1901.

Levi, Leoni. *Wages and Earnings of the Working Classes. Report to Sir Arthur Bass, M.P.* London, 1885.

Lloyd, Trevor. *The General Election of 1880*. Oxford, 1968.

Lockwood, David. *The Blackcoated Worker: A Study in Class Consciousness*. London, 1958.

London, Jack. *The People of the Abyss*. London, 1903.

Lynd, Helen Merrell. *England in the Eighteen-Eighties*. London, 1968.

McKenzie, F.A. *Famishing London—A Study of the Unemployed and Unemployable*. London, 1903.

Mackail, John. *Life of William Morris.* 2 Vols. London, 1899.

Mann, Tom. *Tom Mann's Memoirs.* London, 1923.

Marriott, J.A.R. *England Since Waterloo 1815-1900.* London, 1913.

_____. *Modern England (1885-1932): A History of My Own Times.* London, 1934.

Mather, F.C. *Public Order in the Age of the Chartists.* New York, 1967.

Mayhew, Henry. *London Labour and the London Poor.* 4 Vols. London, 1862.

Mearns, Andrew. "Outcast London," *The Contemporary Review,* XLIV (December, 1883), 924-933.

Mill, John Stuart. *Autobiography.* New York. 1873.

Morley, John. *The Life of William Ewart Gladstone.* 3 Vols. London, 1903.

_____. *Studies in Conduct.* London, 1867.

Newsome, David. *Godliness and Good Learning: Four Studies of a Victorian Ideal.* London, 1961.

O'Broin, Leon. *Fenian Fever: An Anglo-American Dilemma.* New York, 1971.

O'Leary, Cornelius. *The Elimination of Corrupt Practices in British Elections 1868-1911.* Oxford, 1962.

Park, J.H. *The English Reform Bill of 1867.* New York, 1920.

Pearson, Michael. *The £5 Virgins.* New York, 1972.

Peek, Francis. "The Workless, the Thriftless, and the Worthless," *The Contemporary Review,* LIII (January, 1888), 39-52; (February, 1888), 276-285.

Pelling, Henry. *Modern Britain 1885-1955.* Edinburgh, 1960.

Petrie, Sir Charles. *The Victorians.* New York, 1961.

Postgate, Raymond. *How to Make a Revolution.* New York, 1934.

_____. *Life of George Lansbury.* London, 1951.

_____. *A Pocket History of the British Working Class.* Tillicoultry, Scotland, 1942.

Potter, Beatrice. "Dock Life of East London," *The Nineteenth Century,* XXI (October, 1887), 483-499.

Protestant Evangelical Mission and Electoral Union. *Report of the Trial of Mr. George Mackay, Containing the Full Text of the Morality of Romish Devotion or The Confessional Unmasked.* London, 1870.

Reith, Charles. *The British Police and the Democratic Ideal.* Oxford, 1943.

_____. *A New Study of Police History.* London, 1956.

_____. *A Short History of the British Police.* London, 1948.

Rowntree, Benjamin. *Poverty A Study of Town Life.* London, 1901.

Rudé, George. "The Study of Popular Disturbances in the 'Pre-Industrial' Age," *Historical Studies,* X (May, 1960), 457-469.

Saunders, William. *The New Parliament:1880.* London, 1880.

Sherwell, Arthur. *Life in West London.* London, 1897.

Sims, George R. *How the Poor Live and Horrible London.* London, 1898.

Smith, E.A. "The Election Agent in English Politics 1734-1832," *English Historical Review,* LXXIV, 1969.

Smith, Francis B. *The Making of the Second Reform Bill.* Cambridge, 1966.

Smith, Paul. *Disraelian Conservatism and Social Reform.* London, 1967.

Somervell, D.C. *English Thought in the Nineteenth Century.* London, 1929.

Soutter, Francis. *Recollections of A Labour Pioneer*. London, 1923.

Spender, J.A., and Asquith, Cyril. *Life of Lord Oxford and Asquith*. London, 1932.

Spyers, Thomas. *The Labour Question an Epitome of the Evidence and the Report of the Royal Commission on Labour*. London, 1894.

Stafford, Ann. *A Match to Fire the Thames*. London, 1961.

Stansky, Peter (ed.). *The Victorian Revolution: Government and Society in Victoria's Britain*. New York, 1973.

Stewart, William. *J. Keir Hardie*. London, 1921.

Thompson, David. *England in the Nineteenth Century*. New York, 1950.

Tillett, Benjamin. *Memories and Reflections*. London, 1931.

Torr, Dona. *Tom Mann and His Times*. 2 Vols. London, 1956.

Traill, H.D., and Mann, J.S. (eds.). *Social England*. Vol. VI. London, 1901.

Trevelyan, G.M. *British History in the Nineteenth Century and After (1782-1919)*. New ed. London, 1948.

_____. *Life of John Bright*. London, 1925.

Tribe, David. *President Charles Bradlaugh, M.P.* London, 1971.

Tsuzuki, Chushichi, *H.M. Hyndman and British Socialism*. Oxford, 1961.

Vincent, J.R. *Pollbooks: How Victorians Voted*. London, 1967.

Walpole, Spencer, *The History of Twenty-Five Years*. 4 Vols. London, 1904.

_____. *The Life of Lord John Russell*. London, 1889.

Watson, Bernard. *A Hundred Years' War: The Salvation Army*. London, 1968.

Watson, J. Steven. *The Reign of George III 1760-1815*. Vol. XII of *The Oxford History of England*. Cambridge, England, 1948.

Waugh, Benjamin. "Street Children," *The Contemporary Review*, LIII (June, 1888), 825-835.

Wearmouth, R.F. *Methodism and the Common People of the Eighteenth Century*. London, 1945.

_____. *Some Working Class Movements of the Nineteenth Century*. London, 1948.

Webb, Sidney and Beatrice. *The History of Trade Unionism*. London, 1896.

White, Arnold. *Problems of a Great City*. London, 1887.

Williams, David. *Keeping the Peace: The Police and Public Order*. London, 1967.

_____. *The Rebecca Riots: A Study in Agrarian Discontent*. Cardiff, 1955.

Wingfield-Stratford, E. *The Victorian Sunset*. New York, 1932.

Woodward, Sir Llewellyn. *The Age of Reform 1815-1870*. Vol. XIII of *The Oxford History of England*. Oxford, 1962.

Young, G.M. *Victorian England: Portrait of an Age*. Oxford, 1936.

_____. *Victorian Essays*. London, 1962.

INDEX